MW00830167

THE HEALING JOURNEY

Relationships Health and Wellness Guide

ROSENNA BAKARI

Karibu Publishing

First Edition

Published by Karibu Publishing

Garden City, New York

ISBN 978-0-9971699-3-5

Also by Rosenna Bakari

- Self-love: Developing and Maintaining Self-esteem for the Black Woman
- Tree Leaves: Breaking the Fall of the Loud Silence
- Original Sin: Understanding the Movement toward Female Agency
- Too Much Love is Not Enough: A Memoir of Childhood Sexual Abuse
- Painting a Thousand Words: Poems for Love to Return Home

Contents

June

July

August

September

October

November

December

The Ultimate Healing Journey

About the Author

Dr. Rosenna Bakari, a Philadelphia native, is the author of six books related to emotional resilience. But, even as a psychologist, she had to develop self-understanding. She had to come to know herself deeply to heal from childhood trauma. Poetry helped her find her voice and she used it as a testing ground to break norms, accept responsibility for healing, and find emotional strength.

She earned her Ph.D. in Psychology from the University of Northern Colorado and has been teaching at the university level for over 20 years. She has presented at professional conferences such as Telehealth, American Education Research Association, and the American Counseling Association. She earned a B.S. degree from Cornell University and Master's degree from The State University of New York at 22 years old. She is on a mission to shift psychology from a focus on mental illness to mental wellness and break down barriers to wellness resources.

As an empowerment expert, she works with clients worldwide using one-on-one and group platforms to support life changes, help resolve trauma, and reset healthy life narratives. She bases her practice on an 8-week empowerment curriculum she developed. Many of the activities she uses are included in this book, "The Healing Journey."

Dr. Bakari cherishes her family more than anything. Her adult children still travel the world with her and her husband of 30 years. She currently lives on the east coast where she continues to write, teach, and empower others to live their best lives.

Other titles by Dr. Bakari include : Self Love: Developing and Maintaining Self-esteem for the Black Woman (1996); Tree Leaves: Breaking the Fall of the Loud Silence (2016); Original Sin: Understanding the Movement toward Female Agency (2016); Too Much Love is Not Enough: A Memoir of Childhood Sexual Abuse (2018); and Painting a Thousand Words: Poems for Love to Return Home (2019).

Foreword

I met Dr. Rosenna Bakari in an online room about relationships. I'm pretty savvy about relationships and have studied how the brain responds to love and relationships for a long time. So, not much gives me that "aha!" feeling. But when I heard Dr. Bakari speak about the different ways couples use one another for emotional arousal she changed the way I thought about some aspects of my research. I was glad that we got to share more platforms because I enjoy hearing her expertise.

When she asked me to write the forward for her book on relationships, my first thought was that I was thrilled that the world would know more about her expertise. Dr. Bakari has figured out how to make people understand where they are in relationships. She has a kind way of getting people to take responsibility for how their actions influence their relationships.

This book is about people looking at themselves. Then they can place where they are in their relationships. I know that this book represents years of the work that Dr. Bakari has been doing. Her occupational wisdom shows in the exercises she offers for each month. She brings in the heart, mind and spirit for readers to measure themselves. Looking in the mirror, writing letters, listening to meditation, and more are going to make something click inside of a person. Reading this book will lead you to see a part of yourself that you didn't realize was influencing your relationships.

People need new messages because too many relationships have failed using the old messages. *The Healing Journey* offers new messages while dissecting why the old messages haven't worked in a long time. High-conflict relationships can be resolved if people are willing to use this guide to question their outdated or misguided approach to love and intimacy.

Dr. Ryeal Simms, Neuroscience
Relationship Scientist

Preface

Welcome to the healing journey. You will learn a lot about my life through the readings in this workbook. But, I may know a little more about you than you think.

Let's see. You want to improve some aspects of your life. You tend to want more than what people are willing to give and get less than you think you deserve. Given your history, you consider yourself blessed to have gotten this far. However, deep inside, you want to feel better about yourself, the world, and others.

The truth is, change feels scary and difficult. You have invested in products to help you reach your goals but still haven't accomplished them. You may desire more money, higher self-esteem, healthy relationships, or a body that makes you feel good about yourself. Yet, despite your efforts, you keep falling short of achieving what you want. You either try to convince yourself that "good enough" is okay, or you find yourself in an endless chase of an elusive goal. Meanwhile, you are left feeling sad, angry, irritated, or agitated. So, you habitually overeat, drink, or spend money to self-soothe. You seek validation from others and experience high levels of conflict in your relationships.

I get it — the insatiability. Nothing fulfills you and you're always seeking more. I used to be that way, too. I did not always wake up each morning with joy and fall asleep peacefully each night. If I weren't making significant accomplishments, I didn't feel worthy of happiness. I believed I had to earn happiness. I did not know I could choose it.

My self-love should never have been determined by how much money I made or the level of my family's acceptance of me. The healing journey taught me that joy derived from materialism or others' approval is fleeting. Like a gallon of milk, happiness gained through external sources runs out and cannot be stored long-term. Eventually, you will have to buy more.

The COVID-19 pandemic starkly illustrated the human dependency on external satisfaction. When people's access to their addictions to wealth, politics, love, and religion were cut off, depression and anger quickly arose. Millions of people risked their lives and the lives of loved ones to access satisfaction outside of themselves.

This guide offers permission to stop chasing happiness and the space to learn how to trust yourself to create it. The readings, critical reflections, and self-awareness activities support personal empowerment transformation. When you take the work seriously without rushing through it, you will feel a shift within yourself and your relationships.

This book should not replace or substitute professional help; it should complement it. If you are working with a professional on mental wellness, consult with them before diving into this work. If the book triggers feelings of depression or anxiety, consider seeking professional help before continuing.

Although I have a Ph.D. in psychology, I do not diagnose or treat mental illness. I specialize in empowerment and transformation by working with individuals to strengthen their wellness.

Are you ready to trust yourself to transform and create happiness from an empowered place? If so, let the work begin.

Warmly,

Rosenna

Acknowledgments

For every person who has been touched by my words, I have felt your reflection and used it to write the next line. For every person who has invested in my wellbeing, I have received you in love. I cannot acknowledge one without acknowledging all. I am grateful for all.

Introduction

Relational dissatisfaction is one of the tell-tale signs of internal dysfunction. Therefore, this book will focus on wellness and relationships. People with high resilience are often able to perform occupationally and appear well physically. However, when emotional wounds linger, healthy relationships are difficult to maintain. When a person has unmet needs, they may have difficulty finding supportive friends and experience high-conflict partnerships, disgruntled co-workers, emotionally distant children, and social anxiety. People often seek help with these relationships without ever addressing the underlying issue: unhealed trauma.

The unhealed heart looks to external forces to assign blame, such as hurtful people or an unjust world. While your trauma may have occurred during childhood, acceptance of personal responsibility is what allows for healing in adulthood. It is our job, not that of another adult, to provide ourselves comfort and safety. Accepting responsibility is the key that will open the portal to our most beautiful, empowered self.

Many trauma survivors look for someone to save them from their pain, and when they think they have found that person, they tend to quickly attach themselves. Fearing abandonment, we cling to those who make us laugh, feel special, or invite us deeper into their lives. We often confuse our feeling of clinginess with love. It isn't love; the attachment is based on fear and weighs heavily on the relationship. As a result, the person to whom we have attached often ends up leaving. The vulnerability of trauma survivors often leads to attraction to the wrong people, inappropriate engagement, and/or sabotaging quality relationships. Sometimes people show up in our lives through the cracks of our dysfunction and are never worthy of space they take up. A repeat cycle of dysfunctional relationships occurs as we navigate heartbreak after heartbreak after heartbreak. The only thing that will stop the vicious cycle is genuinely loving ourselves more than we love anyone else and more than we expect anyone else to love us.

There is nothing wrong with being hungry for love. We just have to learn to cook for ourselves. We can be needy too, but we have to learn to self-soothe. Healing is self-loving and self-soothing. While healing is not a linear progression, the healing journey has identifiable phases as it relates to relationships: *Denial, Disclosure, Deindividuation, Discovery, and Development.* Each phase attracts and repels certain types of relationships.

In the **Denial** phase, survivors minimize the effect of trauma on their current life and do not identify as survivors. Perhaps they have achieved a degree of external success that disconnects them from the internal trauma. They may think highly of their skills and achievements and believe others are to blame when something goes wrong.

Some survivors in denial tend to care for others as evidence of their humanity. They play the role of caregiver or martyr to connect with others. They may consider themselves empaths and take on the hurt of others instead of dealing with their own pain. High-conflict relationships are often built in the denial phase, where trauma survivors are attracted to the trauma of others. Other survivors in the denial phase numb themselves and feel nothing about other people's pain. They do not pursue attachment at all. Emotional independence is their emblem of survival; lack of vulnerability becomes their identity.

Going within does not happen in denial. Survivors lack an understanding of internal processing. The concept may seem illogical for a survivor who has achieved success and cares deeply for others. All of their efforts to navigate the world are based on external awareness and response.

During **Disclosure**, survivors tend to attract other survivors as they seek validation of their hurt. The goal is understanding, not healing. Survivors in this phase are looking for "secret-keepers." Unfortunately, relationships between survivors become toxic if both partners do not move beyond the disclosure phase. If only one of the survivors moves beyond the disclosure phase, they may outgrow the relationship, leaving the other partner repeating a cycle of victim abandonment.

In the **Deindividuation** phase, survivors look to be saved instead of saving others. They identify themselves primarily as survivors, filter every aspect of their lives through the lens of a survivor, and set up all of their relationships to revolve around being a survivor.

Survivors in this phase are looking for support from a specific person to show up in their lives. This comes with a great deal of disappointment because survivors cannot find people whose commitment to them is as strong as their commitment to others. I sabotaged many friendships by giving them the task of being a support person in my life. Regrettably, I always returned to a feeling of isolation.

When we get stuck on our need to heal and use it to engage in relationships, we sell ourselves short. We end up sabotaging instead of developing healthy relationships. Even when we attract healthy people, they don't stay because healthy people don't want to be counselors to their friends. Healthy relationships are not meant to help us heal but to live. Bitterness, resentment, and self-righteousness are common in this phase, and many survivors do not find their way out of the negativity.

In the **Discovery** phase, survivors move beyond the survivor experience as their primary identification. We expand the boundaries of friendships and take on the responsibility of self-love and self-discovery. What we once expected of others, we have learned to give to ourselves.

In this phase, survivors begin to develop various compatible relationships instead of looking for people who offer validation. We attract good human beings who are kind, appreciate diversity, have a sense of humor, show reciprocity, and minimize dysfunction. It is a bonus if they are self-aware, socially conscientious, highly emotionally intelligent, and spiritual. Those traits may be our personal calling of transformation, but not our mission. Healing should make our world bigger, not smaller. Our hearts must remain open.

We usually meet good people while engaging in activities that we enjoy, and therefore, we know we share something in common. We don't meet just one of these people; we meet a variety of them depending on the expansion of our lives. If we only go to church, we will only meet religious people, not necessarily spiritual ones. If we only go to the gym, we will primarily associate with people who share body vanity, not necessarily quality health. If our primary socialization is the bar…well, that's where we will find partying buddies, not necessarily friends.

However, the more variety we have in our lives, the more varied our friendships will be. We won't have to rely solely on one friendship because we will have a network of friends. We may have a friend who makes us laugh and act silly, a friend for serious talks, one who knows the answer to every question, and one who knows everybody. We don't stop exploring friendships after finding one person we vibe with and who is willing to spend time with us. As we learn ourselves, we discover more friendships. We learn that we are not one-dimensional but complex human beings, and our relationships should reflect that. When they do, we move to the development phase.

In the **Development** phase, the survivor commits their life to personal development. We try to see people as they are and not how we want them to be. We attract people, then choose how to engage them without a survivor script. Healing is a lifelong journey where we meet people along the way. The length of each person's journey varies. So, we must leave room in our lives for people to enter and exit because we no longer take people hostage nor allow ourselves to be one. Our relationships have little conflict as we ultimately understand that every relationship is a relationship with ourselves.

～

I heard a Knock at the Door

One morning I heard a knock at my door
The tap sounded familiar,
Like I'd heard it before
Soft and light like a timid child
Asking me to come out and play for a while

But I surely didn't have time to play
So I just waited for the child to go away

Around noon after I'd finished my chores
Rap-a-tap tap was again at my door
This time too loud to be ignored
My – this little girl must be bored
I sat sipping my coffee as I yelled...,
"Not today sweetie"
Hoping she would just go and play freely
Didn't she know I have a grown-up life
I'm a professional, a mother and a wife
I don't have any time to waste
I have to keep up my grownup pace

Just when I thought I'd gotten rid of the lad
I heard a knock that somehow sounded sad
The child must not be wanting me for a game
Maybe I should invite her in, and ask her name
On second thought,
I can't afford the distraction
And I probably can't give her any satisfaction

Eventually she'll tire and go back home
So I decided to just leave her alone
I turned up my music so I couldn't hear
There was no time to worry about her tears

I'd cry myself if I had time to weep
But I can barely set aside enough hours to sleep

And that night when I finally went to bed
I took two pills to get the day's troubles out of my head
But before I could drift off to sleep
I heard a knock at the door, along with a weep
I sat up in bed thinking that child must be lost
She'll get me to the door at any cost
Ugly thoughts ran through my head
As I rolled out of my queen Victorian bed
I know she's only a child,
But she's making me mad
I'm not her mother… and where is her dad?

One hand on the door and the other on my hip
I opened the door just a little bit
But I didn't see anyone so I opened it wide
No child in sight so I walked outside
I checked for shadows by the street light
No sign of a child, just the silent night
Perplexed, I came back in the house
The knock sounded so soft,
Maybe it was a mouse

Maybe I should have opened the door the first time
Or at least when I heard the child whine
She may have been in trouble and needed to be saved
I could have at least looked out of the window and
    waved
Even if I didn't have time for a game
Couldn't I at least have asked her name
Did she run away because she knew how I would
    respond
That my words to her would have been unkind

I occasionally questioned if a knock is what I heard
And always wished I'd responded with kind words

I'd just about given up completely
When I finally heard the sound so sweetly
Rap-a-tap tap softly at my door
I stopped right in the middle of my chore

With a smile on my face and my arms stretched wide
I was ready to invite the little girl inside
But as soon as I opened the door
To welcome my little friend
I realized…
The knock was coming from within

January

Self-care is Self-centered and Necessary

Taking care of yourself is the greatest love you can show to others. Although love requires sacrifice, including compromising time, energy, and resources, it does not require selflessness. Sacrificing self-care and joy should not be an expectation for love. People often neglect their physical and mental needs to contribute to someone else's quality of life. They make unhealthy sacrifices for their families, employers, or social groups in ways that leave them too depleted for self-care.

Every year, people renew and then break their promises to take better care of themselves. They wake up just early enough to focus on their family's morning routine or get to work on time to impress their boss. Entrepreneurs can be the worst culprits of selflessness. Some self-employed go years without clocking out; every minute of life is part of their hustle.

How society thinks about wellbeing may be part of the problem. The value of relationships is over-emphasized or misrepresented. Indeed, humans are social creatures, and *survival* depends on how relationships are cultivated. However, humans are also spiritual beings, and *wellness* depends on the relationship they develop with themselves. Ultimately, there is a desire to move past survival to truly living well. Living well is about one's relationship with self, not just relationships with others.

According to the Danish web publication *The World Counts,* well-being has five dimensions: positive emotion, engagement, relationships, meaning, and achievement. This perspective is limiting. True happiness requires self-care, and self-care requires placing significant boundaries on those very dimensions. The five identified dimensions of wellness can be a contradiction to self-care.

Self-care often requires decisions that do not always lead to immediate *positive emotions*. Ending unhealthy relationships, pursuing higher education, and healing childhood wounds do not result in immediate positive emotions. The positive effect is a long-term outcome brought on by a continued growth lifestyle. *Engagement* and *relationships* can become barriers to looking inward. Hearing the voices of society, family, and echoes of success while silencing their inner voice will take them further away from themselves. Those voices rarely point in the direction of self-care; the survivor will be called to try harder and give more. Finding *meaning* and *achievement*, when pursued externally, leave people little room to honor the person they currently are. There is always more to achieve. If a person makes their life about finding a purpose, it will be lived in distraction.

Few people come to know a life of stillness, where their purpose finds them. Many people make a purpose out of their pain, often exacerbated by a lack of self-care. People can, however, utilize self-care as an invitation for purpose to find them if they take to heart the Norman Kelly phrase, "You can't pour from an empty cup." The more you are required to give to others, the more you must have for yourself.

Once a person has learned how to fill their cup, they become better at pouring into others. When a pitcher is near empty, the lid must be held while turning it upside down to get everything out. Similarly, when humans are operating on empty, emotions get turned upside down, and minds become agitated. Serving soon turns bitter, and attempts are made to sweeten it with perfection. Filled with high expectations and the demands of others, our end results are distractions that become emotional companions.

Self-care is not self-centered, but it is "self" centered. Care should be centered around individual needs before focusing on other people. Incorporating a yearly vacation charged to a credit card and stressing about paying off the bill for the rest of the year is not self-care. Instead, build a life with personal needs and interests at the center — the counterintuitive life. You may think you have too many responsibilities to put yourself at the center of your life. Work, family, organizations, and religious commitments squeeze you out of taking care of your needs, or so you think. In reality, the thing that chokes you out is *not* putting yourself at the center of your life.

Self-care is consistent, not random. It is a way of life, not a mental break, and it requires conscientious gestures, not grand ones. Take time to connect with yourself in joy. Heal your wounds. Old wounds show up in your dreams and whisper to you that you are not enough in all your endeavors. Negative self-talk robs you of self-care and leads you to believe you don't deserve it. Meet yourself where you are and take your mind on a joyride (not in a car.) Find the inner joy that makes you feel like a carefree child. Move your body so you can feel it do something other than transport your brain from one meeting to another or from the car to the couch. Dance and feel your hips sway. Swim and let the water support every ounce of you in love. Climb a mountain and value your strength. Take a yoga class and pay homage to the mind-body connection. Self-care requires a conscious connection to your body, not just your mind.

Unlike a life of sacrifice, which is rarely reciprocated, self-care is contagious. When you model self-care, you offer people permission to do the same. People will need you less, and that is good because the most genuine expression of love is in being valued, not just needed. When you cultivate relationships where each person takes care of their own needs, your relationships will be more fulfilling. Everyone involved will have more to give one another.

Activity One: The Matter of Time

1. List ten weekly activities that you engage in. For example, cleaning the house, working, exercising, attending worship, caring for children, etc.
2. On a scale of 1 to 10, rank the enjoyment you derive from each activity.
3. Fill in the blank for each activity. When I
   _____, I feel _____.
4. Reflect on your responses throughout the month. Try to rearrange how you spend your time to take better care of yourself. Make a plan and put it into action.

January Daily Gems

January 1

The world will not make it easy for you to heal. You will find listeners only through trial and error. You will create safe space by distancing yourself from some of the people you love. You will build confidence by disappointing people. You will move forward by leaving behind beliefs that no longer serve you despite your attachment to them. You will stand out by your willingness to stand alone. Healing is not easy. But neither is perpetually adjusting to a life of pain.

January 2

Learning to love yourself isn't really about learning to love yourself. Self-love is about paying attention to the fear in your life that keeps you too disconnected to honor your soul. You already love yourself, but you cannot access that love because you spend all of your energy trying to hold onto people, places, and things that do not reflect love to you. Accessing self-love is difficult when your focus is on others. Pay attention to the beliefs, behaviors, and boundaries that separate you from your authentic self and begin to notice how things change.

January 3

No matter what you have been told or what you have told yourself in the past, you are enough. Life is better when we operate from a place of knowing that we are enough. Life's not out to get us, no matter how rough things get. We have all that we need to move forward and uplift ourselves. People will disappoint you, and you will rise. You will lose something that you love, and you will still thrive. You will seek and not find, yet you will shine. Why? Because you are enough all by yourself. Everything that brings you joy is an accessory, not a necessity, because you are enough, and your most authentic joy comes from within.

January 4

The healing path is not a paved road. There are no road signs or convenient rest stops with clean bathrooms to relieve yourself. The journey is a hidden dirt road with sharp turns off the main highway, noticed only by the gaps in the tree line. Cars are not allowed. Travelers stroll, accompanied only by trees and streams of water. The trees bear fruit to feed you, and the flow of water will cleanse you. The fellow passengers will encourage you to keep walking, but you must find your own path. You will get lost now and then which is OK because peace is the only real destination.

January 5

In the face of adversity, our instinct is often to throw a pity party or a tantrum. For our hyper-alert brains that have survived dysfunctional environments since childhood, that makes sense. However, healing requires us to interrupt the pity party or tantrum and look for a green light in another direction. Conflict, disappointment, and regret push us to the places that fear would not otherwise let us go. The work requires you to trust the process, stop waiting for all the red lights to turn green, and head down a different street instead.

January 6

If you love your body, you will find great pleasure in and through it. If you do not, you may find great pain. When you are in tune with it, your body can be your compass. A smell can trigger emotions; your eyes draw attraction, your ears yield compassion, your tongue beckons for pleasure without guilt or shame. When you do not love your body, you ignore its messages. You are prone to overeat, drink too much, and sexualize yourself as a bargaining tool for love. Instead of numbing the body with food or alcohol, you can offer yourself the pleasure of a massage, a bath, or a workout routine. Allow your body to be seen and touched by others without fear or judgment. Love your body to free your mind.

January 7

Observe your behavior with a sense of responsibility rather than judgment. When we feel judged, even by ourselves, the brain reacts with a survival response, and we become defensive. We grow when we see our potential to be better than we are right now, not when we see ourselves as inadequate, insufficient, or lacking. A growth mindset permits us to risk, change, and strive for more while loving ourselves just the way we are. We are never the flaw. We are the one that witnesses the flaw.

January 8

Love offers emotional security. When the heart finds a home, people can take responsible risks and feel supported. However, security in a relationship should not determine security within ourselves. Ask not what your partner can do for you but what you can do for yourself. Rework your interest in getting people to love you better by figuring out how to love yourself better. Show people how to love you by showing up for yourself in love. After all, people can't make us happy, but they can mirror the happiness we have within.

January 9

Experiencing the pain did not break you. Holding on to the pain will not make you. Living free of pain does not deny its essence. Our resilience can never exonerate anyone who wronged us. So, process what it means for you to live free. Work through the rough patches of the past as they arise. Keep working, but allow the pain to diminish as it does. Be careful not to hold onto what no longer serves a positive purpose. Pain is not a badge of honor. And calling ourselves healed isn't a badge of honor either. It's all just our life experiences. Peace comes in being present in our experiences, not in the labels we place on ourselves or our experiences.

January 10

We avoid healing the most by avoiding our feelings. When we permit ourselves to feel whatever comes up — pain, anger, surprise, love, acceptance, forgiveness, aloneness, etc., we honor our emotions instead of masking them. Unpleasant emotions surface to be healed. When we refuse to feel the uncomfortable emotions, we miss opportunities to heal. We can trust our emotions when we allow all of them to provide information about where we are on our journey. As we heal, we feel. As we feel, we heal.

January 11

No matter how evolved, conscious, saved, or developed a person may be, pain should be explored and trauma should be addressed. Trying to hide, ignore, or deny pain does not help a person move on. It is tempting to pretend you have moved on to satisfy the world, but what happens on the inside is of grave importance. Unaddressed fear, insecurity, and rage create an imbalance that will show up in a matter of time. Healing invites us to pay attention and be present no matter what shows up.

January 12

Moving forward on the healing journey and living in our truth may require us to restrict contact with our dysfunctional families. However, if we fill the void with other dysfunctional relationships or unhealthy behavior patterns, we will not move forward after all. For every action, there is a reaction. Life is a constant motion of making the next right decision. Life does not change because we make one great decision, but because we make conscious choices habitually as an ongoing commitment to healing.

January 13

We may temporarily avoid pain by ignoring circumstances but end up numb, realizing our whole life has been built around the pain. Unfortunately, we set ourselves up for the "compounded pain effect." When pain experienced during regular life comes our way, as it does, it attaches to the denied pain. We cannot avoid job losses, losing people to death, children leaving home, or economic crashes. The longer we live, the more experience we have with pain. However, healing allows us to move through the pain without suffering.

January 14

Healing is a rebirth, so do not be afraid to start from scratch. You are pregnant with possibility. You have labored a long time in survival mode. Now you are ready to learn to thrive. Give birth to the new you and raise your consciousness. Nurture yourself with the attention you would give to a newborn baby.

January 15

High-quality relationships have patterns. One partner is never guessing how the other one feels about the relationship. Some signs of a healthy relationship include taking the initiative to spend quality time together without demanding it. Happy couples resolve conflict in a way that feels good and never degrades. Decisions about the relationship are based on respect, not fear. When one partner becomes a hostage in the relationship, these characteristics are often absent. The length of a relationship is not as important as the quality of a relationship. We need to continually take inventory of our relationships.

January 16

Every ending is a new beginning. So, do not allow fear of losing something to keep you holding onto the dysfunction. Look for new birth, new opportunities to grow and develop. You have to take a new path to get to a new place in your life. You determine the course, the pace, and the mode of transportation, but you must move. You must leave something behind, let some things go, and change. Sometimes the willingness to embrace change is the biggest difference we can make.

January 17

Healthy people have a sense of humor, though they find no humor in degrading or hurting other people. Healthy people like to have time and space for themselves. They desire companionship, not an adult-sitter. Healthy people bring out the strengths in those around them. They do not berate others for their weakness or attempt to drain their power. Most importantly, healthy people are attracted to healthy people. In turn, we must become healthy people to begin attracting healthy people. Keep in mind, being healthy does not ensure they will stay in our lives forever. Healthy people move on when the time comes.

January 18

We cannot heal ourselves and taunt those who are different from us. We cannot seek empathy and scorn others who seek it. We are neither better nor worse in our life challenges. Sometimes, what we seek is what we need to give.

January 19

The answers we get in life are only as good as the questions we ask. When we do not ask questions, we tend to take solutions of convenience. The problem with convenient answers is that they are usually more convenient for others than for you. Religion, family, politics, and cultural education all provide solutions of convenience for us. We are taught not to ask questions in these systems. We uphold these systems with our unconditional loyalty. If we ask a question of transformation, our understanding of these systems shifts drastically. "Who benefits from these expectations?" is one such question.

January 20

Healthy people tend to attract other healthy people. Dysfunctional patterns tend to attract similar behaviors. If you are having difficulty attracting the type of people in your life that you want, consider the practices you are using to attract them. Raise your vibration by hanging out in spaces where people manifest and create. Attend art performances, take a class, join a sports team or volunteer in an organization. Make yourself visible while giving yourself people to choose to invite into your life.

January 21

Emotions, while vital, should not be your guiding force. Unresolved trauma leads to unresolved emotions. So, our emotions beckon for our attention to resolve what was unaddressed. Emotions do not tell us what is right or wrong. Emotions signal us to heal what was left unattended. *Feeling* unlovable doesn't mean you are. *Feeling* like someone mistreated you doesn't necessarily mean they did. *Feeling* like someone loves you doesn't necessarily mean they do. Emotions are not meant to override logical evidence of reality. The brain is supposed to work in tandem with the heart.

January 22

Being alone is unsatisfying, and being with people is annoying. Even when you get what you asked for, you wish you had asked for something else. You feel that happiness is always just beyond your reach. Perpetual discontent is common for survivors. You have to invite peace. Stop searching and stop resisting. Just keep inviting in peace. Train your mind to yearn for inner peace.

January 23

Healing is a lifelong journey and requires great effort. The unhealed mind is impossible to satisfy, standing at attention while watching for flaws, prepared for conflict, and seeking perfection in yourself or others. It operates from a position of "lack" instead of love. The healing path, however, teaches us to focus on love rather than lack. In love, we learn to be patient with ourselves and our progress. We do not need to be any further along the path than where we are today. We can be here without judgment and without identifying as lacking.

January 24

If everyone treated you just the way you wanted, life would be fantastic. You would not have to make any decisions or create any boundaries for yourself. In essence, everyone else would be responsible for your happiness. You would never have to enforce boundaries or stand up for yourself. Unfortunately, relationships don't come with a guarantee that you will not get hurt. At some point, everyone will need to create boundaries to guard their hearts and deal with rejection. Making these choices is active participation in life. If you passively participate, you only get to be on the receiving end of rejection, boundary-setting, and risk-taking, and life hurts a whole lot more under those conditions. In healthy relationships, people create boundaries that let people in and out of our lives.

January 25

You are in control of your life. However, you can't control the outcome. Outcomes vary according to luck, resources, experience, and the amount of work you put in. Resources are the hardest to obtain in that formula. To build your resources, you need knowledge. Fortunately, knowledge is relatively easy to come by these days if you put in the work. Read books, articles, and ask for information. Repeat the process as many times as necessary to build the resources you need. Stop thinking that healing is all emotional work. It's also a straight-up grind. Learning, learning, learning, and doing, doing, doing. Be active in the healing process.

January 26

Where shame exists, feelings of insignificance are triggered frequently. When there is a feeling of insignificance, people tend to live their life trying to counteract that feeling. They overwork themselves or over-attach to people who make them feel significant, even if in dysfunctional ways. They look for significance outside of themselves, ultimately, subjecting themselves to the power of others instead of acting on their own power. The key to taking back power is healing shame with consistent internal work.

January 27

Much of healing is learning how to live with the imperfection of ourselves and others. It is possible to know peace even while we struggle. We can learn to love while we surrender to what we cannot control. Sometimes, in learning these lessons, we resort to old patterns for comfort or familiarity. But, even resorting to old patterns of comfort in desperate times is part of our growth. There is back and forth in our new behaviors before we become consistent. We grow into personal power, not perfection.

January 28

The part of us that produces the negative self-talk is not the same part of us that listens to the negative self-talk. Like standing in front of a mirror, the image that you see in the mirror is not you. If you are in a store's dressing room, you can view yourself in a three-way mirror and see your front, back, and side at the same time. Still, none of the images are you, they are simply images of you. The same goes for the inside. The three voices reflecting you are not you. You are the person who watches the reflections. How you interact with the reflections matters.

January 29

When we are triggered, our emotional alarm system is trying to get our attention. It is saying, "Hey, over here! Heal this!" Too often, instead of leaning in, we run away. Imagine running out of the house because our smoke detector went off but leaving something burning on the stove. Usually, we would turn off the stove, open the windows, and decide whether the pan can be cleaned or must be thrown away. If we run out of the house, the fire will grow and eventually burn down the house. In the same way, a trigger does not mean our emotional house is burning down. We have to tend to whatever is on the stove. Open the window and let in some fresh air. The "fresh air" may involve a night out at the movies, taking a hiatus from social media, an extra workout or yoga class, or something else to help us breathe in some positivity. When we hear the alarm, we should try not to panic and lean in instead.

January 30

The mind loves to be right. Our minds use emotional defenses to make us believe we are right even when we aren't. Being right feels safe when we are used to being punished or shamed for being wrong. The need to be right can keep us in constant conflict with others, as well as distant from ourselves. If we are only willing to be right, our minds will deny or justify when we are wrong. No growth can occur under those circumstances. We grow when we challenge ourselves to see the world differently than how our mind has organized it.

January 31

Practice truth-telling because the truth can set you free. No one owns your truth. Do not sell it for acceptance or a feeling of worthiness. You own your truth. Just like owning a car, no one can tell you where to drive it. You are behind the steering wheel. You do not need permission to disclose your truth. Whenever you choose to speak your truth, do it in honor of freedom, not for validation or affirmation.

February

How to Apologize

People often assert, "I'm my worst enemy." However, psychology research tells us differently. The truth is, when making excuses for bad behavior, people are kinder to themselves than they are to other people. Even if we feel guilty about bad behavior, we are unlikely to admit our wrongdoings to others. Our human tendency is to justify or explain our bad behavior to manage people's impressions of us. As social creatures, we are motivated to elicit happy feelings and avoid negative emotions associated with us.

As if we don't have enough evolutionary incentive to maintain a good impression, the lifestyle in the United States is based on the behaviorist model, punishing even the smallest unwanted behavior. This model was deeply embedded during slavery. The slightest attempt at autonomy was met with severe physical and psychological assault on captured Africans. Upon entry to this land ruled by white supremacy, immigrants also quickly adapted to this system of punishment and reward. These patterns of our past are the blueprints to our current inability to admit when we are wrong.

This insidious model of punishment and reward also undergirds our primary methods of raising children. We have long been taught to punish children physically and utilize shame to elicit "good behavior."

Good behavior is obedience and loyalty in the U.S. cultural system. In psychology, we refer to the system of reward and punishment based on obedience as the behaviorist model. It is so deeply embedded in the U.S. that most citizens will do anything to avoid admitting they are wrong. Unfortunately, we sometimes cause more damage trying to be right than admitting when we are wrong.

In the name of appearing "right," religious organizations fail to address sexual abuse. Police forces fail to address police brutality. Medical institutions fail to address common malpractice. Instead of addressing the wrongs, institutions shift the focus to what is right within these systems. Instead of apologizing for what is wrong, they continue to justify their actions. What our major institutions get wrong, individuals also struggle to do right. Leaders of the church, police force, and medical field could say, "I'm sorry we have abused our power," and employ reasonable measures to regain the community's trust. Then, shut up and listen to their constituents. Authority doesn't need to defend itself because it is already the authority.

Unfortunately, adults in authority were likely raised in an authoritarian lifestyle. Perhaps our leaders regularly attended religious services that reminded them that God would punish them too. Despite being dysfunctional, these systems get recycled because appearing good is more important than *being* good. We can't change systems without changing people.

Learning to deliver a heartfelt apology is an often-overlooked necessity of humanity. Since the actions we take at the personal level are the same actions we take at systemic levels, we have to become better individuals if we want better systems. As long as we are trying to manage and control others, we must pretend to be perfect and hide all mistakes. Only when we've been backed into a corner, and apologizing is our last defense, do we make an apology. Intentions are misplaced. Offering an apology to get people to do what we want is not an apology at all. It is a trick, gaslighting, and manipulation.

We should apologize to give the other person what they deserve, an extension of our humanity, recognition that we could have behaved better, and a commitment to do better next time. Being authentic and transparent is the key to quality relationships, not being right and mighty. A genuine apology should create space for redemption. The offender must offer space for the other person to heal their heart, which may require temporary or permanent time, space, and/or distance. The offended party is free to choose their response based on their needs, not those of the offender.

An apology is not a request for forgiveness; however, a request for forgiveness requires an apology. An apology should be offered independently of all other requests and must not be an attempt to manipulate behavior. Most apologies end with redemption if the offense is not egregious. Be mindful that people often need time to self-soothe, even after an apology is made. Make sure you apologize from your heart, not your ego. If your ego is involved, you will wait impatiently for a positive response to your good deed. Be careful; your impatience may position you for the need for another apology.

Some people never offer redemption. I spent five years in my twenties dating a person who scolded me for anything that went wrong: a bad day at school, a flat tire, and all his sadness. I had no room to make honest mistakes in that relationship. Eventually, I realized that I deserved redemption and made the decision to leave. Making an apology should not make you a scapegoat. If you are in a relationship in which there is no redemption, you must ask yourself why you are there. What beliefs are you holding that keep you committed to a relationship without redemption? It doesn't matter if the relationship is a job, a friendship, or a spouse. For many people, unresolved trauma keeps them where they don't want to be. As we heal, we must operate to find compatibility, not permanence.

Show up with authenticity and transparency and see who you attract. That will reduce the need to apologize in the first place. Still, we will hurt someone someday, no matter our efforts toward kindness. We cannot please everyone, and we make mistakes even when we try our best. That's the nature of being human. When you do need to apologize, keep these tips in mind:

• *Listen more than you talk.* When someone expresses to you that you have caused pain, let them know you hear them. Hear all that they have to say. Avoid defensiveness, as it will likely shut the person down and keep them from telling you the whole story. When the hurt individual does not feel heard, bitterness may remain, even if you apologize. Try to understand the entire story before you say a word to defend yourself or apologize.

- *Be specific about the infraction.* If you allow the person to tell the entire story, you know exactly how to apologize. "I'm sorry I didn't come to your dinner party" is more effective than "I'm sorry I upset you." The former acknowledges your actions. The latter focuses on the person's response to your behavior. The former is more effective.

- *Take full responsibility.* Be conscious not to make your apology contingent on the other person being willing to take as much responsibility as you. Contingency apologies end more relationships than they save. You don't need to wait to take responsibility for your actions. That's why it's best to focus on your actions that offended the person and not the person's response. Do not expect your apology to trigger an equal sentiment.

- *Allow consequences.* Apologies should not be designed to make amends with another person. Show up with authenticity and transparency and let nature take its course. In many cases, a deeper bond will happen. In some cases, nothing happens. But keep in mind that no relationship ends because an apology took place. Relationships end because of the infractions that lead to the apology. You really have nothing to lose.

You may feel worse after you apologize, especially if the apology is not accepted right away. This feeling is normal. It's your ego reminding you that vulnerability is dangerous. After a while, if you examine your discomfort, that lie will fade. Even a well-delivered, heartfelt apology doesn't repair all hurt feelings. If you overturn your apology by demanding forgiveness, you have missed the point. Let people make their decisions according to their needs while you figure out your needs. Trying to trap people into a relationship with you is never a need; it's manipulation and control. Don't do that.

Activity Two: Being Sorry

Think about a person who you are willing to admit that you hurt, then do the following:

1. Write out the action you did to cause hurt to the person with as much detail as possible.

2. Write out the point when you realized that you were causing harm. For example, if you knew you were wrong but thought you would not be found out, then state that you knew from the beginning. If you knew because the person explained to you that you hurt them, then note "When you explained to me…"

3. Write what you did when you realized that you were responsible for causing hurt to the person. What were your thoughts, emotions, and actions?

4. Write why you do or don't want to apologize to the person.

5. ONLY WRITE your apology to the person. Do <u>not</u> give it to the person. This is only an exercise.

6. After you have completed steps 1-5, reread the article and assess how well your letter aligns with the tips for an authentic apology.

7. Sit with the letter for a minimum of 48 hours before you determine if you wish to use it as an offering of apology.

8. Share the letter with someone you trust, but not the person to

whom you wrote the letter. Ask for feedback. Take what is helpful and leave the rest. Do not try to explain or justify yourself. Just receive the feedback.

9. Hold onto the letter for another few days while you continue to edit and contemplate. Then you may decide to 1) give the person the letter, 2) keep the letter to yourself and have a verbal conversation instead, or 3) have no communication at all.

February Daily Gems

February 1

Birds of a feather flock together. Research has supported that adage. Victims tend to help victims on the healing journey, survivors gravitate toward survivors, and thrivers attract one another. Thrivers are not likely to settle into a life with people stuck in victim mode, as victims are not capable of reciprocation. Build your resilience so that you draw strong people to you.

February 2

Appreciate the resilience of your inner child, the child that experienced trauma and had to figure out a way to survive while living in a world that felt unsafe, unpredictable, or unjust. That child figured out how to survive. Now, your adult self must figure out how to thrive and make the inner child feel safe and loved. The child had the resiliency to survive an unhealthy environment, and now you must have the resiliency to create a healthy one.

February 3

Healing is counter-intuitive. What we do to escape the discomfort is not what heals us. We want to be isolated but spending time with people can lift depression. We tense up and become more aggressive with people but laughter lightens the heart. We stay glued to the television or computer but turning off the invasion of negative influence will better protect us. We rely on outward comfort, addictions, food, drugs, alcohol, or relationships, but going within will offer us clarity. Because healing is so contrary to our living patterns, we must make a conscious choice to learn all we can about the healing journey and commit to doing all we can for ourselves as we travel. Healing is a decision that requires work.

February 4

Most people do not want to go within and see the work that is theirs to do because they haven't learned how to live without judgment. If they go within and see something that needs work, they beat themselves up. They do the same to others, tending to lead with judgment instead of compassion. They have strict ideas of how the world should work and how people should live. They do not value the complexity of the world. So, going within is difficult because the self is complex. Noticing the work that needs to be done is not about becoming worthy or lovable. We are already those things. It is about becoming authentic and empowered.

February 5

Burdened by fear and hurt, people seek dominance and control over other people. Personal power becomes a defense instead of a tool for peace. People who pursue power as a defense rather than seek it for personal growth remain stuck in a cycle of emotional pain. Instead of building a quality life, they operate in survival mode by seeking power. Survival is the opposite of personal power. Creating peace with others from a place of personal power is where the true potential lies.

February 6

One sign that we are not in our body is that we find ways to disconnect from it physically. We do not look at or touch ourselves. So how can we take proper care of ourselves? The mirror can be an essential healing tool. Look at yourself in the mirror and touch yourself. You can use touch by applying lotion to your body or taking extra care to dry off as you pat yourself dry. Dress in front of the mirror. Use positive words along with the experience. If you do not feel positive, then say the words that you want others to think about you as you look at and touch yourself.

February 7

Most of your fears have already come true and what you are holding onto is a lie. If you live with a fear of rejection, you likely have been rejected and twisted your life to hide the pain. If you live with the fear of failure, you have already failed to be your authentic self. Your fear of abandonment arose from your past, the past that you have already survived. What awaits you on your healing journey is a reintroduction to your resilience. The healing path will not destroy you. It will restore you.

February 8

Acceptance is a prerequisite for healing. We must come out of denial and be present to the reality that we were once victims. Some of us were so hell-bent on surviving that we've never accepted that truth. Instead, we rejected all vulnerability, ran from any potential of getting hurt, and refused to take risks. We can acknowledge that we were once young, vulnerable, and victimized. Instead of overcoming victimization by denying harm, we can choose to accept past vulnerability and hurt. Healing is not possible without acknowledgment. Acceptance is the beginning of the healing journey, not the end.

February 9

If you find yourself in a relationship in which a person does not look out for your best interest, walk away. You will not die. You will live better because you will not live in fear of them leaving. You will stop spending so much energy on pleasing behaviors. You will use the energy you save on yourself. Instead of trying to fulfill another's needs, you can work on fulfilling your own needs. You can find peace in *doing* rather than anxiety in *waiting*. Dare to trust yourself.

February 10

Trauma imposed by humans is not part of a necessary life continuum, not when created by humans beyond our survival needs. No one needs to be harmed as a child to be strong as an adult. People who survive trauma are not better than people who have never experienced trauma. We can heal from trauma without giving trauma power in our lives. The truth is that trauma does not bring out the best in humans. Injury compromises wellness in every area. Those of us who thrive after trauma must be careful not to glorify the trauma. When trauma is glorified, those who die from trauma are inadvertently blamed. Instead, we should work to stop those who create the trauma.

February 11

Wherever you are in your healing journey, advancing to the next level will involve what feels like a dip, where the trauma becomes more evident because your weaknesses show more than your strengths. Embrace the dip and its discomfort with trust and confidence that the solution is found in being present. As we harness the energy of the dip, we will come out of it with more strength and confidence, not an accumulation of stories about how life is unfair. Growing our wings of compassion in the dip instead of having them clipped by fear will help us maneuver the many dips on our healing journey. We can then use them to grow rather than regret them as setbacks.

February 12

Negative self-talk is embedded in old scripts about ourselves that we've attached to our identity. Those attachments are not easily broken by reversing sentences from negative to positive. To effectively change our self-talk, we have to be present and get to the root of the judgment. We must learn to watch the internal judgment without reacting, knowing that the voice is simply a part of a dysfunctional past. If we can better understand the voice from the past that is showing up in the present, we can grow. We must not be in a hurry to change without first taking time to understand.

February 13

We have the potential to be our best no matter how bad our past was. The marker of resilience resides in us, enabling us to capitalize on our fearlessness to change the world and our lives. Instead of asking what we could have been, ask what we will become despite the trauma. Trauma does not erase our potential for greatness. We just have to work harder while building our resilience. Nothing we do now will be more complicated than what we survived as children.

February 14

Many people who've had adverse childhood experiences become experts in learning how to struggle and win. We pride ourselves on overcoming adversity. We become great at the struggle, so much so that we invest in struggling more than we invest in healing. We push ourselves as martyrs, do-gooders, and empaths, unaware that we have simply become addicted to struggle. Pain becomes our only teacher. But, if we can observe this pattern in ourselves, we can shift from "overcoming" to healing.

February 15

The relationship that you build with yourself will guide the relationships that you make in the world. The less you trust yourself, the more space you leave for others to take care of you. So, you find yourself trying to manage your relationships with other people instead of managing your relationship with "self." Focusing on your relationships with others seems like the right thing since society puts so much importance on relationships. So, focusing on self is counter-intuitive. You have to develop the power to be your own guide. When you trust yourself, you stop worrying about how people will treat you or accept you. Instead, you build competence and confidence that emphasize self-acceptance.

February 16

Learning to love ourselves genuinely is the best defense to avoid dysfunctional symbols of love. Convincing someone that they cannot live without you and you cannot live without them is not a sign of love but a sign of grooming. Someone taking care of all your needs while isolating you from the world is not an act of love but an act of grooming. Someone hurting you because they do not want you to leave is not showing love. It shows that you have been groomed for pain. Bad people seek victims who are seeking love. Do not be the victim of "love".

February 17

Humans have become so far removed from our universal divine knowing that we accept pain as a tool for learning. We don't know how to change without it, but change dictated only by pain is a dysfunctional pattern of living. Healing brings us back to the divine, where there is a way of living and learning that does not require pain. Learning requires stillness, consciousness, cooperation, and empathy. We must believe that we can grow without pain. Where pain already exists, we must give ourselves permission to release that pain and find other ways to feel alive. Pain is not our nature; it is our inheritance. We can gently say, "No, thank you."

February 18

We must sit comfortably in the learner's seat. We sometimes give our epiphanies away too fast, turn to teacher mode too soon, become the preacher instead of the choir. Healing takes time and internal focus. Moving along the journey requires insights to create inner change, and not change the world. When internal change collects among the masses, the world will change. As you change, you can invite people into your world of change. You are the one who must do something with the messages of change that you receive.

February 19

Isolation comes easy for many people living with deep emotional pain. We isolate, sometimes physically, often emotionally. When we shut down to feel safe, we miss out on the opportunity to heal, because growth requires taking risks. Strength can often be found in risk and vulnerability. While isolation may feel safe, healing will not likely occur. The ability to take care of yourself is crucial, but there is a difference between isolation and living authentically and transparently.

February 20

Situations do not produce feelings, but past experiences can trigger feelings about current conditions. The earlier we are into the healing journey, the more accurate this is. As we heal, the past has less and less effect on our present responses. Instead of the mind full of fear and pain, the heart begins to respond. The soul lives from a place of peace and love, and not the temporary peace that comes from ignoring pain or avoiding conflict. The heart holds pure love, knows no lack, and has no fear. It exists only in the present and does not attach to the past or future. The heart is "present-tense."

February 21

People in pain tend to complain a lot, and we have plenty to complain about. Many of us seem to have gotten an extra serving of adversity in life. Nevertheless, complaining does not heal the heart. Instead, we must lean into grieving. Complaining is external, but grieving is internal, and we know that healing is an inside job. Even though we are taught to complain and are discouraged from grieving, the opposites are required for healing. Grieving is not the same as feeling sorry for ourselves. Grieving is allowing the pain to wash over us as we honor what was lost and taken. We cry, mourn, process, and we grow. Grieving does not make us weak; it makes us whole.

February 22

The pain you find on the healing path is not the same pain you experience in denial. Pain on the healing path is a side effect of your brave choice to change your course of living. Finding your voice can echo back pain as you work to construct your narrative. The isolation you experience from setting boundaries can evoke self-doubt. The uncertainty you face can produce anxiety. These pain points are leading to freedom. A needle in your arm makes the same prick, but whether the syringe was filled with insulin or anesthesia makes a big difference in the outcome. So, do not give up on the healing journey because you're experiencing unwanted feelings. Trust the process, and the outcome will matter.

February 23

The most critical components of an environment for a child's brain to healthily develop are consistency, safety, and predictability. These characteristics allow children to learn healthy attachments, take risks, and build competence and confidence. The absence of these character-istics diverts the child's brain development to focus on threats and live out of fear; fear of abandonment, harm, or isolation. We have to be active in healing, reading, thinking, learning, and practicing stillness to redirect our brains toward healthy attachments and risk-taking. This work represents "re-parenting" ourselves.

February 24

Windows represent opportunities to make different decisions than we previously made. Life's windows open and close all the time. When we are disappointed, we should look for the window. Rather than leaning into regret, we can climb through the window. When we feel unfulfilled, the window will appear. Windows dare us to choose a place of self-love instead of fear. Windows lead us to the truth. Every time we let the window close, we return to living the lies. When we are ready to live our truth, we will welcome the open window.

February 25

Are you "all-in"? Ready to use your mind instead of letting your mind use you? The mind lives off history. Emotional defenses prepare you for tomorrow based on what you experienced yesterday. That is the most basic use of the brain. However, if you do not want your tomorrow to look like yesterday, you have to use intention to train your brain to work differently. You will learn to look back for lessons without attaching to familiar dysfunction. You will have the ability to think about the past to determine boundaries without living in paralyzing fear. You will grow to mourn the past without yielding to feelings of powerlessness. On the healing journey, feed your mind, train your thoughts with intention, and be all in.

February 26

Through healing, we learn the difference between giving and sharing, when and what to give, and when and what to share. In desperation, we give, give, give, in the hope of getting something in return. We give our bodies in hope of love; we give love in hope of safety; we give money in hope of friendship; we give time in hope of acceptance.

Often, the only thing we get in return is disappointment if our intentions are misplaced. Giving requires nothing of the receiver. Make sure your giving is without expectation and your sharing has clarity of boundaries.

February 27

Resist the urge to react every time you feel discomfort, do not like the consequence, do not get what you want, or feel a lack. When we react, we bring energy into the negative situation and stir things up. We become unknowingly addicted to stirred-up emotion. The intense emotions make them feel alive, noticed, and validated. So, the mind seeks to react to external stimuli, leaving no need to go within. This complex cycle is difficult to see and harder to stop. The only way to raise our level of self-awareness is to go within. Focus on observing the cycle. The energy of observation, combined with desire and intent, is a magical power on the healing path.

February 28

Your inner child is so much more than a space of vulnerability. Childhood is full of creativity and development risks that help us grow. When we bury our inner child, we often bury those aspects of ourselves. We stop cultivating experiences that help us grow. We live our adult lives miserably safe and stagnant instead of taking creative risks. Remember that the child survived. Reconnecting with your inner child is a necessary step toward thriving. Honor your inner child to free your adult minds.

February 29

In the name of culture, family, or religion, we are often made to believe that other people are more important than we are. Respect for authority, kindness to strangers, and protection of family are noble ideals indeed. Unfortunately, those values often become obstacles to healing. Healing requires us to risk, resist, and reject much of what we ascribed to as children and into adulthood. Noble ideals work within an honorable environment. Many of us have only experienced dysfunctional environments. Now, we must pay attention to our internal environment, become the authority to respect, be kind to ourselves, and protect our boundaries. In the name of healing, we do these things.

March

How to Build Relationships
When You Don't Trust People

We love comeback stories. We take inspiration from those who beat the odds. Our motivation comes from people who continued their efforts in the face of likely failure. We realize the challenge of turning a ship around. Sure enough, turning mistrust into trust is no small feat. The level of trust we employ to navigate the world is related to early feedback in our childhood environment. Several theories tell us that trust is the cornerstone of quality child-rearing. Children rely on healthy adults to love, guide, and rescue them when needed. When trust between adults and children remains intact, children are likely to develop into healthy adults.

Unfortunately, research on adverse childhood experiences shows that more than 20% of the population has at least one childhood circumstance that may have compromised the quality of adult caring they received. The list of common negative childhood experiences includes having a household member with mental illness, criminal activity, or addiction to drugs. Of course, a child's victimization of emotional, physical, or sexual abuse is also a significant disruption in normal development.

Childhood experiences may make negotiating relationships in adulthood difficult. For example, children raised in high-conflict homes may not trust their ability to resolve conflict as adults. A child of divorced parents may develop abandonment issues. Neither of the above situations involves intentional harming of the child, yet the consequences are lasting. As social creatures born at the mercy of adults who are supposed to care for us, trust or mistrust is a function of child development.

As children, we learn to trust adults before we learn to trust ourselves. When adults respond to children with kindness, care, and safety, they know we have given the appropriate signals. This caring exchange of message-and-response is how we learn to trust ourselves. As we develop trust with ourselves, we learn to create boundaries and value the boundaries of others. We allow for disappointment in relationships and use healthy communication to resolve conflict.

When all goes well during childhood development, we use relationships to express joy, not create it. On the other hand, we enter the school of hard knocks when, as adults, we unconsciously rely on relationships to fill in the gaps of our childhood emotional needs. Rather than experiencing people authentically, we try to predict who can fulfill particular roles for us, and relationships end before they begin.

Trusting ourselves allows us to make decisions about relationships based on who people are rather than who we want them to be. If everyone behaved as we thought they should, we would not need boundaries. We wouldn't have to choose who to share life with or how because everything would work out. At the mercy of adults, children need to behave to be safe. Adults, on the other hand, need to enforce boundaries to be safe. Adults are only at the mercy of those to whom they give their power. If we give away power, we will feel like victims. The key to not feeling like a victim is to take responsibility for keeping our power.

Quality relationships tend to form slowly. People who value themselves tend to create boundaries that take a while to get through. They also respect the boundaries of others, so they do not seek fast relationships. Beware of relationships that develop suddenly. If a relationship feels too good to be true, it probably is. If we can't see the slightest flaws, the person may be hiding them for a good reason. When we feel the exhilaration of a new relationship, we need to advance slowly, no matter how much we appear to have in common with the person. Speed, in and of itself, is exhilarating. Fast cars, roller coasters, airplanes, we love them, but they cannot survive a collision. Neither can fast relationships survive conflict.

Relationships should not start with a destiny, such as marriage or a supporter of your healing journey. Go slow to allow the relationship to evolve or dissolve into an authentic, rather than forced, depth. Someone understanding us is not a willingness to rescue us. Someone making us feel special is not a commitment to love us. A declaration of love does not make someone responsible for our happiness. We have to assess the long-term offering of the relationship as we go.

Assume that the exhilaration from the attention and care offered early in a relationship is the inner child being fed dessert. The inner child is the first to respond to the new and shiny. Let them have fun, but do not relinquish the adult responsibility of relationships to the inner child. The inner child is a flawed negotiator. In the best of relationships, needs are negotiated. Our responsibility is to live in the space of love by fully loving ourselves first. That way, when conflict arises within relationships, we don't respond out of fear that we are unlovable. We are enough because we are enough, not because someone loves us.

Fear of abandonment may get triggered when relationships have conflict. Some people may throw a childish temper tantrum or lash out. Others may respond with childish humility that self-blames to please the other person. There is a better alternative. We can sit with the discomfort, the feeling of threat, the fear that we will never be enough for someone to love us. We can allow fear to become our entry into spiritual development, where we feel so loved by the universe that no void ever exists within us. We must hold space for our fears without following them into dark uncertainty.

Relationships are not possessions; they are significant human experiences. When we learn to trust the experiences that we create, trusting people becomes less problematic. Empowering the inner child keeps us from responding to relationships with fear or becoming an emotional hostage. Empowering the inner child may require letting go of tradition, discovering our way, starting new trends, and adopting beliefs that support our wellbeing. Staying small, quiet, or hidden to feel accepted, as if we were children, leads to a sense of victimization. We must keep reminding ourselves that we are no longer children. We are adults who can make responsible decisions and keep ourselves safe.

Adults who grew up in dysfunctional environments may develop a high endurance for emotional pain, uncertainty, and mistrust. Instead of using pain as a signal to escape, pain may signal a survivor of childhood trauma to try harder. High pain tolerance often keeps people stuck in dysfunctional relationships that recreate their childhood circumstances. Often, people mistake their attachment to familiar pain for love. In truth, love teaches you to let go of everything so that it may teach you how to hold onto anything. The inner child must be re-parented to love like an adult.

The relationship that we develop with ourselves will guide the relationships that we create in the world. No person worthy of our love or friendship wants us to treat them better than we treat ourselves. Emotionally mature people don't invite others to love them who don't love themselves. So, it is necessary to work on building trust with ourselves to attract healthy people into our lives. You can start with affirmations. Writing affirmations on random paper is like leaving ourselves love notes. It is also a good practice to say mantras when going to bed and when waking up. "I am capable of making good decisions, and I will make good ones today." The favored mantra of this year is, "I am enough." Mantras work when applied along with healthy behaviors.

Show up for yourself, especially in the mirror. Research suggests that observing our mirror image increases moral behavior. I imagine that goes for trusting ourselves as well. If we avoid looking at ourselves, we can't expect anyone else to respond to us any better than we respond to ourselves. If we cannot trust ourselves in the mirror, we aren't trusting our relationship with ourselves.

Confidence is built when we invest in ourselves by developing a skill that we are better at than most people. Becoming an expert builds internal trust. Developing expertise requires an investment of personal time as well as confidence. If we cannot identify something that we are better at than the average person, we should find something that interests us and commit ourselves to work to be better at it.

When we build a relationship with someone, whether they're a friend, co-worker, or lover, we must work on not getting caught up in just our feelings. We should evaluate the person's lifestyle early on to assess if it is compatible with ours, remembering that trauma is not a compatibility trait. Building relationships from shared victim stories are initially affirming but frequently a recipe for disappointment. We have greater success when we are open to relationships with people from different demographic backgrounds than us. Our ideal friendship might be with someone twenty years younger or older than us. Our intimate companion may be a different race than us. Our most supportive co-worker might be a different gender orientation than we are. The most compatible person may be the one we least suspect. Make sure you explore their perspective of the world, not just invite them into yours.

Remember that relationships are a reflection of how we see ourselves. How we see ourselves should evolve. If we trust the process, we will not try to hold on to everyone who offers us a pillow to rest our heart or a piece of bread to feed our soul. They may not be meant to travel with us, so the only way for us to keep them is to stop moving on our journey. Room must be left to invite people into our lives and for them to go. Also, we have to give ourselves permission to leave. Fulfilling relationships reflect *how we have shown up* in our lives. Painful relationships expose *our need to show up* in our lives. Every relationship is, ultimately, just a relationship with ourselves.

Activity Three: Nice to Meet You

Think about how you invite people into your life. List the last three people you have invited into your personal life. Write your responses to the following questions and reflect on them.

1. Where and how did you meet them?

2. How long did you take to claim them as someone significant?

3. How did you check in with them about your expectations of the relationship?

4. How did you communicate your expectations in the relationship?

5. How did you create boundaries in the relationship?

6. What is your current fulfillment in the relationship?

Now do this part:

Write a love letter to yourself with the promise to show up for yourself the way you want other people to show up for you. Try to make the letter a full page (300 words). You can write about when you met yourself, what you thought about yourself, how you fell in love with yourself, and how you will continue to love yourself forever.

Notice the ease with which you can identify self-love. If writing a love letter to yourself is difficult, you may be relying too much on others to bring you love and happiness that you should be manifesting for yourself. Just know there is work to be done in that area. Make the promise to do the work for yourself in your letter.

March Daily Gems

March 1

Shame often hides within us, even when we live openly. We are often not conscious that we are working from a place of shame. Shame can cause shyness, decrease our motivation to lead, or keep us from establishing healthy boundaries, all because we want to hide who we are. We build a life of smallness and cramp ourselves into it. The scripts given during our childhood development are vital to staying small and carrying the big shame. No one ever gave you permission to write your own script, much less taught you how. Until you learn, you are stuck with the shame. Adopt the spirit of a child, not the child that you were raised to be, but the child that you are meant to be. The child that is full of responsible risk and curiosity to learn is still within you. The child within is not afraid to love, to lead, or to let go.

March 2

You are enough. Nothing can add to your enoughness. Nor can anyone subtract from it. Let your love be a reflection of your acceptance that you are enough. Don't love others as a filler for self-love. Love doesn't work that way. Just be enough all by yourself. Then, share your enoughness with others. They are neither more nor less than you. You can love them without needing them. You can support them without catering to them. You can respect them without giving yourself to them. Just be enough, and that's enough.

March 3

Do not mourn your choice to heal. Keep making choices that serve your inner child instead of wishing you could be with the people who mistreated you. Be there for your inner child. You do not need relatives' approval more than you need self-care. If you believe that the only way you can heal is for people to give you support, you will spend your time looking for help instead of healing. No one in your life is required to join you on your healing journey. You are the one that life is calling forth. Say yes, and follow the path.

March 4

Rescuing others from their pain will not heal your own. Doing good does make people feel better in general, but, healing isn't about feeling good temporarily. Healing is about operating from a position of personal power where your authentic self is most present. It is about thriving. You make decisions from a place of love instead of a place of fear. You are not afraid to invite people in or let them go because relationships are accessories, not necessities. The most critical relationship is the one you have with yourself when you are healing. That is where you must do the most good.

March 5

Emotional defenses are a natural part of survival. The problem is that they become obstacles to thriving. Healing reveals how we use defense mechanisms to make conscious decisions about our lives rather than unconscious reactions. Eventually, we adopt a healthy understanding of ourselves and our world that empowers us to create, not just react.

March 6

When we are finally called to heal, the calling is like a dog whistle. Only we can hear the silent sound. We begin to see ourselves and the world a little differently. Our thoughts change little by little as we invest in learning, relearning, and unlearning. However, we sometimes make the mistake of forcing the lessons meant for us onto others who are not traveling with us. Your spouse, children, parents, or friends cannot hear the dog whistle. They are not on the journey that you are taking. If you want company, you must find others who have heard the whistle. There are plenty of us in the world who are healing, but many of us follow people who are not, which stagnates us. We choose people with too little care and then try to create a life different from our chosen people. Healing challenges us to decide the type of people we want in our lives and live our lives to attract those people.

March 7

Dealing with your past does not mean you are stuck in the past or living in it. The pain we feel grew with us from the time of our trauma and into the present. The present structure of your brain is hypersensitive to particular experiences. Your inability to manage healthy boundaries is presently real. The isolation you currently feel from letting go of unhealthy relationships is genuine. However, you cannot heal your current state of dysfunction by ignoring the past. Trying to do so is like painting a house that needs a new roof. A fresh coat of paint can be slapped on a house without much prep work, but the only way to repair a roof is to take the old roof off. Similarly, in healing, we must do what is most necessary, not what is most convenient. There is no shame in taking the roof off (revisiting our trauma) to repair our lives.

March 8

You must go first. Whatever you want others to give you, give yourself first. However much you want others to love you, love yourself that much first. However much you desire someone you can trust in your life, trust yourself that much first. Be the person you are waiting for. When you show people what you require by being that good to yourself, others are likely to follow.

March 9

The time comes when the secret you hold can no longer be contained. Dreams are interrupted by the Boogeyman's threats, and days are littered with the anxiety of "what-ifs." Family time is wrought with feeling like a neglected child. Conversations are scattered to avoid disclosure, and silence no longer feels safe. The weight of carrying secrets grows with each passing day. If you are in this space, you cannot go back to your previous state of comfort. The only way through this hell is to move forward and destroy the darkness by allowing truth to shine through. Holding onto the secret no longer serves you. Let go.

March 10

Finding your voice is not an act of rebellion. You have the right to be heard, not just the right to remain silent. You are not responsible for hiding the harm that others do. The fear of telling the truth should not be greater for survivors than for violators. But truth-tellers have been persecuted throughout history. They have been burned as witches, crucified for heresy, lynched for disobedience, and stoned as traitors. The truth is that revolutionary truth has always come with sacrifice. Isolation, name-calling, and denial do not have to stop you. And, your truth may set future generations free.

March 11

You cannot leave your healing up to social media and professionals. You must also seek and use intellectual information. No one person can tell you precisely what you need, nor can they tell you everything relevant to your healing. Some big concepts like "epigenetic" and common themes like co-dependency or some acronyms like ACES and MPD may sound too complicated to learn. But they are not too complex if you invest time. You do not have to learn everything at once, but you have to learn to heal. What you know can influence what you feel and the direction you take on your journey.

March 12

In healthy environments, peace is predictable. When you show up, peace invites you in. In a healthy environment, love is free, not earned. In a healthy environment, adults take care of their own needs. Adults do not hold one another accountable for bringing joy. In healthy environments, a large spectrum of emotions is allowed and expressed. These elements should be apparent in your environment. If they are not, then the environment may be a liability on your healing journey. Rather than commit to the dysfunction, you can try to reconstruct the environment or reposition yourself.

March 13

What your mind tells you is hate for your inner child, is actually fear. Out of fear for their pain, your mind uses the world's dysfunctional scripts to send messages to your inner child. As long as you profess hate for your inner child, you will never live in your truth, for they are your truth. So, look after them and speak gently with love. Carry your inner child close to your heart and listen to the whispers. There is so much brilliance, strength, and creativity in this child who learned to survive so that you could be here today.

March 14

We cannot think our way out of the victim mentality. We must act our way out. Our mind is watching and will feed us the thoughts that coincide with our behavior. Our behaviors will then reinforce the beliefs, and the cycle will continue until something interrupts the pattern. We cannot interrupt our deeply patterned thoughts with more thinking. People who try to do so end up more frustrated. We can only interrupt deeply patterned thoughts with significantly different behaviors. The beliefs that we hold support our behaviors. Changing our behavior interrupts our thought patterns. We have to DO something different. The more drastic the behavior change, the more likely the thought patterns will change.

March 15

Fear of abandonment haunts many people as a result of adverse childhood experiences. If we didn't feel unconditional love or didn't feel like a priority to our caregivers, we tend to carry anxiety about people leaving our lives. Relationship breakups or conflicts hurt us deeply, no matter how much we know we are not at fault or believe we are better off without the person. We are never responding to the current relationship but the first love of our lives—our mother. We can play out the desire to be mothered in so many dysfunctional ways that trigger our fear of abandonment. Each of us must know that we are loved and that we are enough. We were always enough.

March 16

If we wear our pain as a badge, it will become a noose around our neck. We risk strangulation from the inability to shift our heads to see the things around us. We suffocate as the victim-identity cuts off our air supply. Recognizing our victimization is essential to healing, but its purpose is to permit us to find the right tools to heal. Then, as we heal, we widen the path for others to heal, too. Our narrative must speak to our resilience. We disclose our strength as survivors. We do not offer excuses; we offer insight. Healing is not a badge of honor but a commitment to hope.

March 17

When we know our power, we use our resources to create happiness, joy, and peace. We awaken to the opportunity to use our power in the choices we make each day. Often, depression and ill feelings are signals that we are giving away our power. As soon as we stop using our power, it becomes available for auction. Our family, job, children, beliefs, and fears will bid for every ounce of power we do not use. Our time, money, interests, investments, and commitments will work on someone else's behalf as we wonder why healing is so hard. Healing is challenging, but healing without power is impossible.

March 18

When we have practiced denial and avoidance, ordinary pains bring extraordinary grief. Every new pain that arises attaches to the avoided pain. We cannot deal with the new pain without revisiting the old pain. We must heal our most profound sorrow to live our best life so that every other experience is not filtered through that trauma. We must commit to growth rather than a perceived need to be different from who we are. Processing and healing pain purges our hearts so when the next disappointment comes, our hearts won't burst from overload.

March 19

The duration of the relationship between a victim and their therapist does not determine how far along they are on the healing path. The number of days per week spent in worship does not determine our resilience. The number of years we remain married is not a measure of wellbeing. Sometimes we exalt ourselves by some external action instead of committing to the internal work required to grow peace and wellness. Freedom from fear and anxiety, detachment from expectations and control over others, and acceptance of the intertwining of pain and purpose are more accurate measures of how far along we are on the healing path.

March 20

To heal the mind without healing the heart will not eliminate suffering. We can treat the mind with medication, meditation, and various distractions but remain in a small world. We learn to transcribe our negative thoughts to positive affirmations, create boundaries that no one can cross, and remove toxic people from our lives. We played it by the book, but it was someone else's book. The sadness and loneliness remain, our faith in the world diminished. Our heart is unhealed, but we call it strength because we don't need anyone. We forgot that we still need peace. Peace is not the absence of pain. Peace is peace.

March 21

We do not move forward by letting go of the past. It is like trying to pull out of a tight parking space by pushing the gas. It just won't work! The tighter the parking space, the more times it is necessary to back up before the wheel can be turned enough to get out. Similarly, the smaller we have made our lives to remain parked in our favorite spot, the more we will have to return to our past. We inch away from the past to avoid careless damage to the things around us. However, we must go in reverse. We must turn our heads fully, stretching our necks to get a good look and assess what is behind us. Only then can we navigate through it.

March 22

Our brains are capable of responding to more than one emotion at a time. The brain also processes conflicting feelings quite expertly. We don't need to ignore internal stimuli to maintain a constant state of positive emotion. Ignoring internal stimuli is a coping mechanism, but accumulating too much unexpressed emotion becomes stifling. Every emotion can and should be explored healthily. We should allow ourselves to feel all of our feelings.

March 23

Healing starts with the intention to do so. When you have the intention to heal, healing is in progress, no matter how slow. But working with intention is not simple. Intention necessarily involves the responsibility of action. Many people never develop the intention to heal. Instead, they have the intention not to feel pain, the intention to save relationships, or the intention to feel loved. These can all be contrary to the intention to heal. When we heal, those other things eventually come into our lives. However, only the intention to heal brings healing.

March 24

Maybe you learned at an early age the advantages of being unseen. Perhaps there was just too much emotional noise to have been seen, or bad things happened when you were visible. You learned to be invisible to move through your environment, to feel safe or accepted. Invisibility became your superpower. No matter how much being invisible has helped you to get where you are, it will not help you to get where you are going. You must be willing to let go of what is no longer serving you. Work yourself out of the comfort of invisibility. Admit to yourself that being seen is the only way to get to where you will do the most good.

March 25

There is a point on the healing path where we become acutely aware of what we need to release to move forward. We also understand that giving "it" up is going to deepen our pain. Let go of the birth family who chooses denial or scapegoating enabled by our silence.

Leave the spouse who never attended to our needs because we made ourselves so small. Stop chasing children who do not respect our efforts to support them. Quit the job that will never allow us time for introspection, much less healing. Let go of the secret we have been holding onto because appearing healed has been more critical than actually healing. The moment we realize what "it" is, is the moment pain rushes in. What we do with that pain matters most.

March 26

We often keep doing what hasn't worked for us because the brain caters to familiarity. We call the same person, go to the same places, and do the same things, yet hope for different results. Healing requires other actions to break cycles of dysfunction. Start by inviting different people into your life. Join a theatre group, a gym, a yoga studio. Go someplace you have not gone before to do something you haven't done. Reach outside of your comfort zone. Travel outside of the country or volunteer for a nonprofit. Explore fresh ways of looking at the world.

March 27

Triggers often leave us with an unidentified feeling of anxiety. We often notice depression but ignore anxiety while it wreaks havoc on relationships. Our need for comfort increases, as does our sensitivity to dissatisfaction. We may unknowingly give mixed messages of "come-close-go-away" as we wrestle with feeling unsafe, unloved, or unwanted. When we go within consistently, we are more likely to notice the small changes that occur when triggered and then better manage our responses. We can realign our hearts by paying attention. The days of discomfort shorten to hours, and the hours shorten to minutes as we build awareness and practice self-soothing when triggered.

March 28

When we lead with our weaknesses, we tend to attract people to our shortcomings. Of course, we attract others' weaknesses, too, rather than their strengths. Relationships based on weaknesses are more vulnerable and less likely to last. Oddly, we often have to struggle alone for a bit until we get to a point where we lead with our strengths. Then we start attracting people to our strengths. If we are having difficulty finding or keeping support, we must continue to heal by focusing on our strengths. Remember that we are never truly alone. We are just in the part of the process that makes us feel alone.

March 29

No matter how much people know about our trauma, people will respond to us according to who they are, not who we are. Understanding pain does not rid people of their painful shortcomings or dysfunctional responses to life. And while we cannot fix people, we may choose to disclose to people, inviting (not forcing) them into a space of vulnerability and authenticity that has the potential to blossom the relationship. Still, we do not get to control the outcome. There are no guarantees, and we must always leave the door open for people to enter and exit.

March 30

Emotions that put us in a dark emotional state can move us forward or mentally paralyze us. Emotions paralyze us when we obsess about how we feel, which is precisely the temptation when we are in the dark space. Our focus becomes narrow with resistance. We become stuck in the thought, "I do not want to feel the way that I feel," caught in a cycle of feeling bad about feeling bad. However, we can train our minds to respond with empowerment instead of resistance. We can honor the dark space as a message to go within. There, we can reconnect to ourselves and find a way to move forward.

March 31

Trust your ability to keep yourself safe. Even if someone tries to exploit or hurt you, you will not let them. You have learned too much and watched too long. You know the ropes better than most. You can remain alert and still be visible and open. Usually, asking questions will provide enough clarity for you to make the best decision that will keep you safe. You can say no to whatever does not feel right.

April

Nobody is Normal, So Just Be Yourself

If we stop trying to be normal, we might be happier. Hopefully, we will never become that person who has given up on being happy and settles for following the social scripts that dictate their life. Some environments discourage us from independent thinking that would give us control over our lives. Expectations within our family, work, and religious systems may be set for us to take few risks. However, we don't get to construct our best lives without risks and independence. Research suggests that a sense of control rather than a sense of conformity may be the key to happiness.

Human beings are social creatures who invest in social "norms." These become informal rules of human behavior used to connect us. When behavior is consistent, predictable, and controllable, we feel stable and resilient. Social norms support social evolution, but social norms are not a moral compass, and individuals come with inherent variances. The owning of human beings and extreme cruel treatment were once a social norm. Women's absence in the political process and the restriction of same-sex relationships were social norms during this century. While these egregious human experiences are no longer the social norm, not every human being advocates for the most humane social evolution. Groups are socially constructed according to shared characteristics, and every group exists within a particular structure of power and privilege.

All social structures change over time, including smaller social systems such as families, organizations, and religious institutions. Given this inevitability of change, fitting in is inherently overrated. Finding a supportive community may serve us better than following the people assigned to us at birth. Pretending to be happy by conforming to social norms will make us more miserable than taking the heat of finding our way. As much as social norms make us feel safe, they can cause us to shrink ourselves emotionally and psychologically. Adults who have experienced childhood trauma may especially desire to fit in and be accepted. Many adults were never permitted as children to take risks without harsh consequences. They learned to succumb to the rules that govern their environment.

Minorities within subcultures may also experience extreme conformity to survive, as being a minority leaves little room for deviating from the norm. For example, being part of a minority race in extracurricular activities or being in a cross-gender career could yield a desire for acceptance.

Social norms fit many people like spandex. Wearing them makes us look better, but we can't breathe too well. We can only wear them for so long before the discomfort becomes overbearing. Girdling ourselves limits our abilities to take in proper sustenance and speak the truth.

The commitment to social norms blocks our ability to process information that conflicts with those norms, forcing us to live in a state of confirmation bias. We take in information that confirms our beliefs and ignore information that confronts our beliefs. In other words, we have to keep our minds small. When we commit to the in-group, we cannot speak out, especially not against those who let us in. The risk of being kicked out is too high. This fear-driven commitment to the in-group is the killer of justice and a get-out-of-jail-free card for bad guys. Bad guys are excellent at embedding themselves within good systems wherein they are protected by loyalty. Social conformity enables bad behavior as easily as it fosters ethical behavior. People are willing to deny the bad to protect the good. Challenging the value of conformity is the norm we truly need.

Normal is defined by people who represent privilege or power, whether considering large social structures, sub-culture structures, or micro-social structures, such as families. Accordingly, children in abusive families often do not know they are being abused until adulthood. Since privilege and power are hoarded, "normal" does not define most people. In actuality, most people don't directly benefit from tightly woven social norms. Consider this non-exhaustive list of some social norms in the Western world:

Education - More is better

Marriage - Reproduction required

Family Engagement - Put family first, especially if you're a woman

Gender Roles - Women nurture; men protect

Politics - Choose a side and stick with it

Money - Save for the future

Religion - Claim one and defend it

Pain - Ignore it

Love - Define it as romantic and pursue it ceaselessly

Race - Identify others by it and self with it

Most people do not benefit from these norms. Education is unaffordable to most people. The divorce rate keeps climbing, politics and religion are equally weaponized, and mental health costs are skyrocketing because people are not supported in healing pain. These norms are not working for a lot of people. Chances are, they are not working for you either. They are not meant to. Our 100 billion brain cells are uniquely connected to design a unique life experience. When we cater to the norms, we make ourselves more invisible, even if we feel more accepted.

Many people are born, raised, or traumatized into norms of disempowerment. They were never allowed opportunities as children to develop a sense of independence. Following social norms often means personal disappointment. Parenting, education, sexuality, gender, religious, and racial scripts guide our lives. We combine these scripts into an identity without questioning the purpose of the scripts or our motivation for maintaining them.

We cannot use our current success as proof that conformity is good for us. We can do more when we trust ourselves. We may have stagnated despite how hard we worked. We may have stopped making goals because our next move would require us to bump up against the norm. We have to work ourselves out of our desire to fit in. No matter how much fitting in has helped us get where we are, it will not help us get to the next level. We must be willing to stand out and make choices about how we are seen.

We have to get out of our own way so people can see us as we are instead of how we perform. We do not just show people the side of us they have affirmed already and share with them our quirks, vulnerability, and mastery that are outside of the norms. We allow people to connect with the real us. Emotional security comes with a price when conformity is our only path. Achieving our hearts' desires is less likely when we commit to conformity instead of ourselves. We should expect to be adored, appreciated, and acknowledged for who we are.

The study of neuroscience informs us that each human being comes pre-wired for certain behaviors, attitudes, and preferences. Our unique human expression should include happiness, which requires working outside of social norms. We need to rewrite scripts, redefine concepts, and re-create narratives daily that support our wellness.

Activity Four: I'm This But Not That

1) Rank order the list of values on the next page from one to ten based on your level of conformity to it. Number ten represents the norm that you are most likely to conform with, and one represents the least valued norm. Ask someone you know to do it with you and have a discussion about your responses.

2) Once you have ranked the list, write about the most significant decision you have made to conform to that social expectation. How does your conformity benefit you? What were the sacrifices, if any, of that decision? Do you regret any decisions you have made to conform?

Value	Expectation	Your Ranking
Education	More is better	
Marriage	Reproduction is required	
Gender Roles	Women nurture, men protect	
Politics	Choose a side and stick to it	
Money	Save it for the future	
Religion	Claim one and defend it	
Pain	Ignore it	
Love	Pursue it ceaselessly	
Race	Identify others by it and self with it	

April Daily Gems

April 1

In an instant gratification era where love has become less patient and kind, successful relationships may prove more difficult than ever before. We must understand that two people cannot become one. One plus one will always equal two. We must accept that sacrifices are never equally made. So, permit yourself to opt-out of the traditional family roles that were designed for survival. Negotiating roles will prevent partners from becoming objects of obligation.

April 2

Disconnection from the body can be difficult to detect. Often, we tell ourselves that a lack of attention to our physical selves is a way of accepting ourselves, but that is our emotional defense talking. Upon deeper analysis, we may find that we avoid exercise not to draw attention to our bodies. We resist wearing accessories, makeup, or revealing clothing to protect against exposure. We generally aim to take up as little physical space in the world as possible to minimize the risk of being seen, but we have no reason to hide. Taking up space in the world and being seen are as much our right as anyone else's.

April 3

Family and "loved ones" are not synonymous. No species on earth is more capable of choosing than human beings. So, we must embrace our power to choose the most critical group of all, "loved ones." Family shares a bloodline. Loved ones are your lifeline. Loving your family does not make them "loved ones" any more than you can make "loved ones" your family. Don't lose your power to your bloodline. Use your power to find your lifelines.

April 4

To disrupt our pattern of seeking, of looking for someone to play a role for us, we must instead fill ourselves with pure self-love. Building a trusting relationship with oneself may take a lifetime. But there is no one to love you better than yourself. We don't need to shift, change, or compromise who we are for people to show us love and acceptance. When we show self-love, people know our value.

April 5

We live a much more empowered life when we define problems in a way that empowers us to solve them. For example, if the problem is defined as "my spouse does not understand me," the spouse will be the problem, and effort will be put into trying to change the spouse. If the situation is defined as "I do not feel connected to my spouse," focus is shifted to finding ways to connect with the spouse that may or may not have anything to do with the spouse's understanding. Many people tend to define problems by looking at others, making the situation more difficult to solve. There is empowerment in defining problems in solvable ways.

April 6

You can't see yourself the way others see you. You have been called rude when you were merely standing up for yourself. Your partner has confronted you about your tone, and you accused them of making you defensive. You can admit that you have little tolerance for people but you justify your impatience, believing people provoke you with their stupidity. As long as you insist on being how you are, never opening up to receive feedback, you cannot grow. You get to decide if and how you will accept feedback from the universe.

April 7

We have to heal our own broken hearts. The difficulty lies in trusting the process. We know we have to cry, but we hold back the tears to hold onto relationships. We know we need to speak but remain silent so that what we say may not be used against us. We understand that we have to go within, but the world's harmful behavior makes us sleep with one eye open. However, to heal our broken heart, we cannot hide for safety.

April 8

If you are waiting for your fear to dissipate before you take the next step in your healing, you may be stuck for a long time. Like a rain cloud on a sunny afternoon, daring us to go on a picnic or a jog, we must take the next step in the presence of fear. Saying no to fear simply means we do not make our decisions from a place of fear. We still risk rejection and failure. But, inherent in every risk of rejection is the possibility of acceptance and success. Rejection and failure are better than stagnation.

April 9

Finding your inner child is part of the healing journey, but nothing magical happens just because we think we have found our inner child. Inner child work is a progression of awareness, a way of understanding ourselves and our lives from a different angle. Initially, that inner child angle is likely to show you a lot more pain than you have been willing to let in at this point. Remember, your inner child has lived through the experience of dysfunction and abuse. When you find your inner child, you re-enter that psychological space. It's like going into a burning house to rescue a child--you will feel the asphyxiation from the smoke.

April 10

Healing of the heart leads us to build healthy relationships. The keyword is *build*, not find. When we are seeking instead of building, we try to win people over. We offer them pieces of ourselves that we cannot get back—our bodies, money, time, and attention. We make these sacrificial offerings, hoping some relationship god will bless us and make this person love us back. But there is no relationship god to protect us. Stay in relationships only as long as they are being built on a foundation of care.

April 11

Where there is a will, there is a way. However, willing is not the same as wanting. Our wants are associated with our minds, our egos, and often they are fleeting. We tend not to work for our desires; we wish for them. Having a will, on the other hand, comes from the heart, not the mind. A will becomes destiny. Working never ceases because you become the will. You build a life around your will. Everything else becomes secondary. Your will becomes more significant than your fears and stronger than your needs. "Will" is how the underdog wins.

April 12

How we see ourselves is reflected in how we see the world. People tend to believe they are kinder than they really are, less judgmental than they actually are, and more generous than they are. We forget about the snarls we give to the person in the mall who is walking too slowly. We justify the impatience we show the cashier that does not ring up the items fast enough. We rationalize the yelling that we do at our children and spouses. We use petty excuses not to tip the waiter and leave harsh comments on social media. These actions are minor tell-tale signs about how we see ourselves. The inside and the outside are related. When wondering how to start healing on the inside, we should start with how we approach the world on the outside.

April 13

Healing is a daily practice. The practice is to remain the center of our own lives and accept full responsibility for how our lives take shape. We all have the resources to build and improve our lives. We may have less money but more time. Maybe we have little time but significant social capital. Perhaps we have great talent that we have not begun to use. Whatever our resources, we need to use them to develop ourselves. Our focus should be on the resource we have in abundance rather than the one in which we have an inadequate supply.

April 14

When you confront your fears of being alone and abandoned, you will find freedom. Given your childhood adversities and the way the adult world operates, your fears are legitimate. However, fear will keep you separated from your peace and your power. The space that you dare to spend in isolation with a sense of rejection is where you can find your most profound self-love. Go courageously into that space.

April 15

If you were forced to grow up fast, you might have missed the opportunity to be a child. You can't be a child again, but you can grow into being child-like. People who are child-like laugh more, stay more active, take more risks, and are more carefree. You can benefit from not taking the world so seriously. Instead of searching exclusively for people who understand and support you, invite people into your life who make you laugh and encourage you to play.

April 16

Feeling bad doesn't mean you are helpless, nor does it have to make you hopeless. Lean into the feeling and ask your inner self for information about your feelings. There is a wealth of information inside of you. Chances are, the emotional pain is pointing you toward something your inner child wants you to know or address. Maybe you are not using your gifts and talents in a way that fulfills you. Perhaps you have not found your voice and the dark space represents your silence. Pay attention to the dark space when it arises. Trust that in it you can access important information that can move you forward.

April 17

Most of us come to the healing path kicking and screaming, wondering how our lives got so out of control. Family issues, health concerns, grief and loss, depression, or some other threat to our comfort finally force us to take a conscious look at our pain. We tried everything we knew in the world of make-believe. We kept quiet, appeared friendly, or lashed out at people to protect ourselves. We tried drugs, obsessive work, workouts, food to console us, but the pain still soaked through our lives. Thriving on the healing path comes after we stop fighting and resisting. Now that we are finally here, let's lean into the journey.

April 18

People are waiting to enter your life that will support your healing journey. They may not be who you've been waiting for to show up, though. They may not share your age group, race or ethnicity, or religion. They may be the least likely suspects for relationships. First, open your heart. Second, expand your mind. Third, use your eyes to see beyond your negative expectations. You may be surprised by all the beautiful people and experiences the universe wants to bring to your healing journey.

April 19

We must offer ourselves forgiveness, not just understanding. There is an endless list of deeds we have justified because of our trauma that has left small amounts of negative energy in our lives. Those small energies accumulate and clog our minds. The point is not to judge ourselves, as judging collects more negative energy. The point is to forgive ourselves. Sincerely acknowledge the pain we may have caused ourselves or other people and create a process of forgiveness. That process may be meditation, fasting, writing a letter, or some other act, but make it conscious and sincere.

April 20

Healing is contingent upon finding our way. Instead of trying to fit in, we start new trends and adopt beliefs that move us forward. We will, at first, live in a state of confusion and unknown territory. It is temporary. A renewed mind requires new actions and new experiences. However, our brain prefers the familiar, so don't expect immediate comfort. It takes time to adjust to the changes we make on this journey.

April 21

Like using a girdle to fit into a dress bought one size too small, we wear our silence, tight enough to make us look good as long as we do not want to breathe adequately. Like the six-inch heels that make our legs look divine, our silence radiates a tremendous personal presentation. No one knows how uncomfortable we are. No one seems to even care as they shower us with accolades about our beauty, brains, and charm. Our minds now plea for our forfeit as the mental exhaustion of the girdle and heels become unbearable. Remove the girdle and find your voice. You deserve to breathe.

April 22

When you jump into a pool, the first minute is uncomfortable. As you start moving, your body adapts. The temperature of the water does not change. Your brain sends signals to the rest of your body to regulate its temperature and minimize discomfort. Similarly, most long-distance runners hate the first mile because the brain takes a few minutes to signal the body to send endorphins. But when the endorphins are activated, they relax into the run. The body can also heal most physical injuries with little intervention, and every time the mind heals the body, information about that healing is stored for future use.

April 23

Anyone who has a personal history of trauma can justify a pattern of hyper-vigilance in relationships. People may view you as arrogant, withdrawn, or defensive. If people are wrong about you, you have to change the way you present yourself in the world. You don't have to be misjudged. If you want to keep people at a distance and use distancing behaviors to do so, then you get to own that behavior. Ultimately, you have to take responsibility for how you show up in the world according to how people respond to you.

April 24

Time is a resource that underwrites our healing. Over time, you should see results from whatever you say you are doing to heal. Over time, we experience more acceptance, peace, direction in our lives, personal responsibility for our joy, less victimization, etc. If you have been "working on healing" for a decade and see no difference in your life, then evaluate, evaluate, evaluate. Do not keep giving your time to what is not working. Change does not usually happen overnight. However, change can be seen and felt over the years. So, if your healing time has not been well spent, then consider a change.

April 25

The world is not black and white. We often make oversimplified observations about the external world that leave us disappointed. In reality, simplistic beliefs will not match our behaviors. Black and white expectations will be inconsistent with our lived experiences. Interpretations without nuance will lead to unreliable predictions. Avoidance of uncertainty leads to conflict over cooperation and emotional distance over support. If we learn to view the external world with greater complexity, we will experience better outcomes.

April 26

Most people take years to connect with their inner child due to the many layers of defenses. When you ask the question, "how do I connect?" the inner child hears the question, then sits back and waits for you to find them. What is between you and your inner child are all the other personas you carry in your head. If you feel hatred towards your inner child, know that the "you" who feels that hatred is not your authentic self. That is only another persona that dominates your life. The "you" who wants to connect with your inner child is your authentic self. Finding the inner child sometimes comes after sorting through several other personas that dictate your life for survival.

April 27

Being resilient is different from being healthy and stable. Our resilience is evident when we discover the healing path. We didn't give up. We survived the trauma and the despair. We are stronger than what happened to us. Yet, many of us are still surviving in critical condition—our scars fresh and open. Some of us are in an emotional coma, while others are (metaphorically) still bleeding internally from the injury. There is more healing to be done. We cannot settle for anything less than our peace and purpose. Keep healing beyond resilience.

April 28

Trauma can be invisible to the eye. Sometimes the evidence is the perpetual sense of dissatisfaction, the feeling of lack, the inability to speak up, a lack of boundaries, or strict boundaries protected by anger and hostility. Fear is the extra weight you carry. Isolation hides the fact that you are taking five medications daily, and you've convinced everyone that you are only a social drinker. You have convinced the world that you are fine while you accept these living conditions. Life can offer you inner peace, nourishing partnerships, good health, and healthy boundaries. But, first, you must let go of your denial.

April 29

When we are so busy loving each other that we cannot challenge each other, too much love is not enough. When silence is our love language, too much love is not enough. When the light at the end of the tunnel is the gravedigger because secrets must be carried there, too much love is not enough. And if too much love is not enough, then there is no such thing as love at all. Love cannot heal a wound no matter how much time pain consumes because love is all you need to cause irreparable damage to a child's faith in themselves so that they will dig their own grave and live there the rest of their life. Any love that directs us to our grave is too much and should be released.

April 30

Healing is not an excuse to misbehave emotionally without accountability or responsibility. Silence in a heated exchange does not indicate victory. Shutting someone up means that you have shut them down. Making others feel like losers doesn't make you a winner. It makes you a victim looking for power still lost. Human engagement is not an athletic competition with winners and losers. No matter where we are in our healing, we must take responsibility for our behavior.

May

When Pain is the Familiar

In the absence of trauma, familiarity helps us develop healthy patterns for negotiating the world. However, familiarity keeps survivors stuck in dysfunctional cycles. It causes us to choose the demons we know over the goddesses we find strange. Ultimately, we maintain tradition because of familiarity, not practicality. The more times any event or experience happens, our brain will likely code it as "normal." The brain codes "normal" according to the reality of the environment, not according to right and wrong. Generally, when a victim cannot stop abuse, the brain will habituate to the abuse to survive, making it "normal."

Adult who experienced severe adverse childhood experiences have a long history of normalizing pain, both internal and external. Attempts at new behavior compete with decades of the familiar. For example, many adults continue to share spaces with people who harmed them as children. The older sibling who emotionally tormented them, the grandfather who sexually violated them, or the mother who physically hurt them may be present at every family function. Although survivors may feel traumatized by sharing spaces with the people who harmed them, they continue to participate. They don't consider making an adult decision to say no to their authority figures. Their brains have normalized the painful experiences.

Survivors can face insurmountable circumstances in fighting the familiar. Breaking their silence typically leads to at least some negative consequences, often steep ones. I was threatened and excommunicated by family members for disclosing my violators in my memoir. Fortunately, I was far enough along in my healing journey not to be disturbed. The family member who threatened me had become reliant on my silence. His brain interpreted me breaking my silence as dysfunction because speaking my truth was an unfamiliar disruption. This is a typical response from family members and often wreaks havoc on the survivor's healing process. Reprogramming the survivor's brain to create a new normal requires extensive internal work. Many survivors are cocooned in environments that support their distortions and misperceptions of the world and themselves. When they start healing and experimenting with healthy behaviors, they are often misunderstood and rejected by people around them.

Changing our familiar usually requires changing our inner circle. While many people attempt to change something small while keeping everything else the same, healing immerses people in change. The easiest way to initiate change is to open ourselves up to new experiences. Instead of convincing ourselves to reject holiday invitations from our family, we can say yes to a friend's holiday invitation. Of course, we must first embrace the part of the healing journey in which we make friends and begin spending time with them.

Change is not simple, and it doesn't occur overnight. I wrote my memoir eight years into my third healing process. Finally, I had built up a network of support, experimented enormously with change, and learned to live with the isolation from my family of origin. I was better prepared for the consequences of writing the memoir than I was for the healing that had led me to that point. Trauma survival is littered with distortions and misconceptions that prevent you from knowing the truth about yourself, your trauma, and the world. Reprogramming requires new experiences that can remap and reroute the brain.

Living in a toxic environment during childhood strips us of the opportunity to discover who we are. Groomed as secret-keepers, enablers, caregivers, and hostages, we learn to focus on others instead of ourselves and center our likes, dislikes, and goals around safety instead of growth. In a dysfunctional environment, safety is misperceived as the conditions in which harm is absent. Children may think if they're not getting into trouble or disappointing people, they're safe. Adults may continue trying to create the conditions for an absence as harm by engaging in perfectionism, hyper-empathy, or numbing behaviors. But avoidance of harm is not the same as safety, and this focus on staying "safe" does not support us in growing into our authentic selves.

Getting to know the familiar parts of ourselves that have always been resourceful, brave, and talented rewires the brain. It may require spending time in new places and doing new things. I started writing almost daily when I began the healing journey. I was discovering a whole new aspect of myself. Once I began exploring my inner child, I had to train my body to stay awake past eleven o'clock to participate in open mic poetry nights. These events often lasted until one o'clock in the morning. A few years into the poetry scene, several people showed me poems I had written that I didn't remember writing. I also found decades-old writing projects that I had forgotten about. I'll never know how much I had written before I knew I was a writer, but I am so glad I rediscovered it. The more I healed, the more I wrote. The more I wrote, the more I healed. Writing to heal was connecting to my inner child.

Going within to find your joy and your laughter will help build a healthy familiar. When the outer world misunderstands or rejects the new you, your inner world must be strong enough and confident enough to continue the restructuring. Permit yourself to experiment instead of expecting to have all of the answers. Learn that life is not a pass-or-fail test. Life consists of trial and error. It requires resilience and tolerance for the unfamiliar. You don't need to go on a fancy, expensive trip to find yourself. You can go to a friend's network meeting that you keep putting off because you hate being around people. You can sleep in on Sunday mornings instead of going to worship because it's what you've always done. Change your grooming patterns. Spend time with people of different races, ages, and sexual orientations—unscript your life. Then strip your life until you get to your most authentic self.

Childhood violation is rarely as simple as one mean adult doing something terrible to a child. When adult survivors begin to heal, they may start with the question, "Who did what to me?" Eventually, they will have to look at the big picture, though. Viewing the big picture of all that occurred for a child to be abused is like emotional cancer to the brain—life-threatening. Coming to terms with all that was wrong in your environment is like walking through hell's fire. Many survivors grow up believing they had an average family despite "this thing that happened to them." I used the word "thing" intentionally because taking the person out of the picture is the first distortion. Survivors perceive the experience of abuse as a thing rather than an action. Many even feel responsible for what happened to them.

Healing means putting family and communities under the microscope to understand the ugly truth. If a child didn't tell, the child didn't feel safe enough to tell. For the adult to heal, they have to understand the dynamics that made living as a child unsafe. They must ask themselves, "Who or what was my guardian(s) guided by that I did not trust disclosing my horror?" Survivors were often betrayed by parents, family members, court systems, religious organizations, and society in ways that were never processed. These iconic networks are protected as unquestionable. When survivors see how these systems have played a part in their victimization, their world begins to crumble, and they find themselves ill-equipped to confront these systems.

But there is a bright side. When we see the roles that systems played in childhood abuse, we can de-individualize our trauma. We see ourselves as part of a problem instead of being the problem. We get distance from our pain with a panoramic view. The way to get this distance is to acquire knowledge—book knowledge, professional knowledge, academic knowledge. The more you know about childhood abuse, the easier it is to reclaim your innocence.

Knowing the resources available to you will serve you well on the lifelong healing journey. You'll need resources about relationships, health and wellness, spirituality, and possibly education and careers.

Making healing wholistic will guard you against stagnation or retreat, especially when you get to the part of your healing that feels more like "helling." To survive, you need only stop your triggers. To thrive, you must become empowered in all areas of your life.

If healing were easy, half of all survivors would not live in silence. Often, the pain doesn't feel worth the effort at first. But, choosing not to heal means never choosing to live fully. Healing may deepen the pain before you can live comfortably in your truth. However, once you are fully planted in your truth, you are unstoppable.

Activity Five: Looking in Your Glass House

1) Write your strengths and weaknesses according to the category in the left column.

2) Find and list your most useful resource to improve your life in that area. Think about literature, websites, organizations, and professionals.

3) Write in the name of a person who you think has great strength in each area. How is their strength exemplified?

Life Area	Strengths	Weakness	Resource	Who is doing it well?
Personality				
Health				
Nutrition				
Relationships				
Career				
Wealth				

May Daily Gems

May 1

Hating any part of self puts strain on the brain and the heart. The brain's job is to keep us alive by signaling danger. If you hate yourself, you confuse the brain as it now has to protect you from yourself. Like having an autoimmune disease, in which the body's confusion between good cells and bad cells destroys proper functioning, self-hatred breaks the heart. The mind cannot tell the good from the bad in your life and often destroys the good via self-sabotage. Commit to practicing love of self. Figuring out what healthy love looks like in your life will allow you to keep healing.

May 2

When there is enough distance between you and your pain, your peripheral vision becomes much bigger. You become acutely aware of how much pain the world produces. When you find your voice, you see the connections between oppression, silence, and pain. Despite our global resources, we are living in a world of unmet needs of human beings. Society has become its own autoimmune disease that cannot tell the difference between the good and bad cells, fighting against itself. May your desire to fit in transform into a desire to fix instead.

May 3

Expressing vulnerability is a strength. When you start a tough conversation by stating how you grew into your perspective, people are more willing to listen. Too often, we express our viewpoint as fact rather than experience. Your experience, even if it was painful, provides insight into your vulnerability. Leading with vulnerability suggests that you are not trying to win. Instead, you are trying to be understood.

May 4

The signs of self-love are the same as the signs that you love others. You enjoy your own company, protect your boundaries, allow room for errors, and speak kindly to yourself. Love does not change its characteristics because its target changes. Love is how we live, not what we seek. Being a good lover of self will make you a great lover of others.

May 5

You do not know how far you can go until you commit to the journey. Do not determine yourself finished, stuck, unable, damaged! In today's world, we know the value of recycling. We, too, can be recycled. Recycle the pain into determination, the betrayal into advocacy, the emotional abuse into resilience, the doubt into wisdom. The recycling process always involves further demolition before rebuilding. So, wherever you are is a great place to start. You are being made into something so beautiful that no one would ever believe where you started.

May 6

Strength allows for vulnerability. Resistance calls for conflict. When you know your power, you can be flexible because you know how to tap into your resilience if anything goes wrong. You draw boundaries out of necessity, not for general protection. When you recognize your strength, you do not need to be hyper-alert. You respond to circumstances as they arise. You do not stand guard. You stand in the present moment, present situation, and present circumstance.

May 7

May is the month when we celebrate Mother's Day. Many survivors have joyful memories to celebrate on Mother's Day, and to you, I say Happy Mother's Day. But many survivors have experienced dysfunctional childhoods and, at best, grew up with a fictionalized version of our family in our head while our hearts hurt. We are still paying the price as we struggle, and often fail, to build healthy relationships with our children, spouses, and friends while continuing to carry feelings of never being enough. To those of us who fall into this category, I say, we are enough. We are doing the best we can with what we were given. We are better today than we were yesterday. Each Mother's Day, let's celebrate our survival and resilience.

May 8

Asking questions keeps communication open. When we feel interrogated by people's questions, it's an invitation to use our voice—to let them know how we feel instead of shutting down. It's a chance to notify them that we prefer dialogue instead of feeling interrogated. If we notice people shutting down when we talk to them, we ought to give them the same opportunity to express it. By putting people at ease, we can learn to turn some questions into personal statements. Building healthy communication skills goes a long way.

May 9

Many people go wrong by trying to build healthy relationships starting from a position of lack. They try to fulfill something they feel they lack instead of offering something they have. Stop assigning people roles to which they have not consented. When we are willing to create and build instead of search, there is no lack in the world. Approach relationships with excitement, knowing that we are not at the mercy of friendship. We are there by choice, not as a captive. When necessary, we can leave, and we can let go because the relationship is not based on lack.

May 10

Silence can be camouflaged as many things, such as forgiveness, success, or even advocacy work. Fear of confronting the past can convince us to claim forgiveness. Shame can motivate us to succeed. In this case, we hope people will judge our book by its cover because the pages are empty—filled with silence. Advocacy work can permit us to use someone else's voice instead of finding our own, trying to live vicariously through the freedom we help others achieve. We may rather be an empath than an outcast, but there is no greater freedom than transforming our trauma into our owned truth.

May 11

When so many people have invested in our silence, it is easy to forget that we deserve to have a voice. Instead of an authentic voice, we create an alternative voice that turns trauma into a denial of self. We deny ourselves the right to be heard, the right to feel safe, the right to heal. We are left with the noise in our heads, confusion in our hearts, and lots of wanting. There is so much to unpack along the healing path. We are capable of challenging the world to listen, challenging ourselves to be listeners, and creating a safe space to be heard.

May 12

If we only pay attention to our healing when triggered, then all we ever do is manage our triggers. Managing pain makes us a survivor, but not a thriver. Surviving does not make for healthy living. It keeps us in reaction mode rather than healing mode. However, when we put healing at the forefront of our lives and pay attention to our internal happenings, we feel the effects of our effort. We count every day as a win because we pay attention to insights, not just pain.

May 13

If the ideal you are holding onto about who you think you should be makes you hurt inside, put it down. Reinvent yourself. Give up what does not work for you. If the person you love refuses to love you with dignity and respect, and that is important to you, let them go. If the job that pays your bills makes you sick and miserable, put it down. Find another way to live. You can reinvent your self-image, learn to live independently, find other jobs, or restructure your life. You can do any of those things, but you cannot get rid of YOU. No matter how much you may not like yourself, you wake up to yourself every day. So instead of taking your misery out on yourself, change what is making you miserable.

May 14

Cycles of unwanted patterns may show up in our lives because we stick with the familiar. We become so good at solving problems, confronting, bouncing back, and surviving that we welcome the practice. When we pride ourselves on being champions of struggle, we may take careless risks, live recklessly, overextend ourselves, or make poor choices. We do not consider the effects because the brain is attached to overcoming negative consequences. We expect things to go wrong, and the bounce back feels powerful. When we have repeated unwanted experiences, we have to look within and figure out our contribution to the experience, not to judge ourselves, but to redirect ourselves.

May 15

The unexamined life is short-lived, no matter how old we get. If we center our lives around victimization, we will miss the fullness of who we are. Victimization is something horrible that happened "to us." If all we ever examine is victimization, we will never know ourselves. Our belief systems, family systems, and social systems play critical roles in how we live and who we become. No matter how painful our experience, those systems should be under constant examination on your healing journey.

May 16

You can be a good daughter and move miles away from your parents. You can be a good spouse and never cook a meal. You can love someone and sever a relationship with them. You can be well educated and highly employable and choose to be a stay-at-home parent. You can do whatever you want and create the life you desire. But first, you must detach from the shoulds and have-tos. Those are for children who depend on others to tell them who they are. You are an adult, rebuilding your life. You don't need permission.

May 17

We benefit when we process our emotions and then choose an action, not the other way around. Too often, we start a cycle of reactions that lead to a dead end. Then we resort to stuffing emotions away instead of processing them. Processing emotions explores the emotion beyond the current situation. Processing may involve thinking about the values and beliefs that provoked the feeling and your history of experiencing that emotion. When we process, we can create a response instead of being taken over by a reaction.

May 18

Trauma is our relationship to past events. Memory cells from the event are currently planted within our brain. So, we are not trying to heal the past; we are trying to heal our current brain patterns. We are not living in the past; the past is living within us. We must reconcile with our past with intention. That may require talking about it, processing it, bringing it to the forefront to understand it. That may involve disclosing to particular people or confronting others. We don't just move on. We heal by moving into the current intersection between our past and our present.

May 19

When we expect and accept that life will be filled with heartbreak, we repeat patterns that yield pain. We miss opportunities to be proactive in creating joy. We become passive instead of active, reactive instead of responsive. We inhabit environments and surround ourselves with people who keep our lives small. Living small may feel like protection or safety because we keep people out, but that keeps us from seeing our enormous potential as we live in the shadows of the few people we do let in. Welcoming more people into our lives does not equate to more pain, and taking more risks does not equate to more failure. They do equate to more opportunities and a deeper investment in the healing journey. As we learn to watch, calculate, and shift, we see our lives begin to fall into place.

May 20

The value of a relationship is not contingent on the willingness of a person to listen to you talk about your history of adverse experiences. You can build relationships with laughter and reciprocity. Quality companions anticipate your needs, like bringing you water to the park even though you didn't ask. They initiate spending time with you and invite you around their family and friends. High-quality people apologize when they are wrong and accept apologies from you. They work to be free of racism and sexism. You are a better person as a result of having these people in your life. As the relationship lasts, people grow into the ability to listen well. So, let those in who will contribute to a high-quality life.

May 21

When we know how to self-soothe, we lose our fear of rejection and take more risks. We do not worry about things not going our way because we know we will be OK. People can disappoint us but not make us fall apart. Situations can cause frustration but not cause despair. We will still experience sadness, anger, depression, and loneliness, but we don't get stuck. Negativity becomes a set of roads that we cross during our journey, but we do not reside in that neighborhood. We become our own therapist, personal trainer, and motivator. We may seek help or advice, but we remain self-sufficient.

May 22

Many people struggle to find success in relationships, seeing them as conflict-driven or void of personal power. To improve relationships, practice people skills without attachment. People skills get us better connections everywhere, not just in our relationships. Smile at people who serve you in any capacity. Speak kindly to people who make mistakes. Make new friends. We too often pressure those closest to us to fulfill our needs for emotional intimacy while passing up a hundred opportunities a day to create emotional connections.

May 23

One part of the healing journey that gets easily overlooked is parenting. So many of us struggle with the shame of unwanted parenting outcomes. We carry many of our childhood emotional insecurities into adulthood. Having never learned healthy attachment, we employ the same unhealthy parenting techniques shown to us. Difficult parenting can yield years of distraction from the healing path. We spin our wheels focusing on our children instead of ourselves. Sometimes we use them as scapegoats, fighting with them rather than facing our childhood trauma. Focus on your healing, and your parenting will improve.

May 24

Life is a creative process. To be creative is to do what has not been done, bring to life what was never imagined, and make visible the impossible. To be creative is to lean into what has already been done, visualize a higher ground, and see the possibility that lies within you. There is nothing more creative than healing the noisy mind. The healing process is creative because you have to transform pain instead of avoiding it.

May 25

There are many ways to find momentum on the healing journey. We can do something to shift how we participate in the world through our body, mind, or spirit. Staying conscious of what we put into the body and how we use the body, we can let go of numbing agents and shift to nourishment. Staying aware of our thoughts and feelings, we can see where our feelings take us as we choose to let them in rather than fighting or avoiding them.

May 26

Sorrow is not our friend, it is our stalker. Despite not being invited, sorrow follows us wherever we go. In a crowd of people having a good time, we catch it staring at us out of the corner of our eye. We keep smiling as we walk through the room, trying to find a safe place to hide. In our home, sorrow sits at the dining table and interrupts conversations. In the bedroom, it turns the sheets cold so we cannot sleep at night. Let not your heart be sorrowful. Greet it with fierce intention. You were not born to live a life of sorrow.

May 27

The brain prefers to respond with "yes" instead of "no." The brain is biased toward the idea of accumulation and resists the idea of loss. Stopping negative behaviors, such as overeating or drinking, is extremely difficult because to the brain, stopping equals a loss. The brain panics over the idea of loss or deprivation. Healing should focus on positive interests that allow you to say yes. Say yes to loving yourself, taking care of your body, finding your voice, letting go of fear, and taking risks to move forward. Say yes to good nutrition, exercise, and meditation. Say yes to education, taking a vacation, or finding a new job. Find the "yes" in your life. Your spirit will thank you.

May 28

Healing comes in layers, not milestones. There is always something beneath the surface. At times, we are in the right place at the right time, and we find ourselves on the fast track. Other times, the next layer is just too difficult to dig into, so we take our time. There is no rush. The onion of healing is not to be sliced but peeled back layer by layer. The more we peel off, the smaller we become—not in a way that makes us insignificant, but in a way that makes us fully open and authentically exposed, living from our core.

May 29

We have been warned not to be seen, told that the spotlight is not for us, taught that the best path is silence and sacrifice. Therefore, we built a life around those standards; be small, be invisible, be quiet. We still play by these rules and blame our problems on others when the rules do not give us results that feel good or help us succeed. But others will never change the rules for us. We must make a conscious decision to live beyond the rules that never served us, no matter how familiar. We must overcome the well-worn thought that we must second-guess ourselves, no matter how afraid we feel. We must reach for something new, no matter how taxed our mind feels.

May 30

We cannot address self-hate with our backs turned on our pain. We cannot heal dysfunction by denying our truth. We cannot restore our vision by closing our eyes to feel safe. When we open ourselves up to the vulnerability of the inner child, the fear of the adult, and the pain that comes with restoration, we begin to heal. Tell me what you are most proud of, then tell me the sacrifices you made to achieve it. Tell me your greatest accomplishment, then tell me the work you put into it. Yes, someone else was responsible for our pain, but we are fully accountable for our restoration, no matter how difficult.

May 31

You are still moving forward. Look at the moon and notice each night how it changes. Sometimes it appears full, half, or quarter. That does that mean the moon is going backward or shrinking. The size of the moon we view depends on its relative position to the earth. The same goes for healing. How much growth you can observe at any given time depends on your relationship to the particular situation. Whenever you see yourself as small, it does not mean that you are going backward or that growth has stopped. It just means that you have a disadvantaged view.

June

How to Get Unstuck

What's more important than safety? Our mind is conditioned to believe, "*Nothing* is more important than safety." If you have experienced trauma, safety feels especially paramount. But when safety is the goal, we miss out on wholistic wellness.

Every human being has needs. We need nutrition to stay alive and we are also social creatures with emotional needs. From the moment we are born and throughout our lifespan, our emotional needs change. Our needs don't change randomly; they change developmentally. Just like there is a cycle of physical growth, there is a cycle of emotional development.

We all rely on one another to get our emotional needs met. Newborn babies rely solely on caregivers. Small children start to interact with relatives, then schoolmates. Young adults begin to experiment with intimate partners. Older adults look for employment that compliments their self-identity.

Psychologist Abraham Maslow used a pyramid to represent psycho-emotional development. Few people advance to the top of the pyramid and get their highest-level needs met. For example, most people have food and shelter, a basis for survival. But not everyone grows up in a safe household.

Even if the household is safe, many people become targets of prejudice and discrimination based on identifiable features or known social status. Fewer people have a deep sense of self-worth and even fewer experience self-actualization.

The pyramid image below represents Maslow's theory about developing into our authentic selves where we master and manifest wellness. My insertions on the left side show how development can get thrown off track.

When safety is the goal, we miss out on the healthy grownup stuff.

The path of optimal emotional development is sometimes interrupted

Cultural Modeling

Coping skills such as numbing or mimicking can mask trauma responses well into adulthood.

Self-actualization

Organized Practices: Religion, economics, gender

Self-worth

Fear of identity expression

Love and Belonging

Historical or generational oppression

Safety

Poverty or neglect

Physiological - Food & Shelter

Understanding Development & Trauma Response

Bakari
MASLOW

Let's compare social development to basketball to get a better understanding. Any kid on the playground can learn to dribble a ball if he hangs out on the basketball court. But, not every kid on the playground will become good enough to make their school team. Out of all the kids who do play on a basketball team, less than 10% will play for a college. And only 1% of those young adults who play for college will get to play professionally.

Maslow believes the percentage of self-actualized humans is equally low. Let's take a closer look at the levels.

- *Physiological needs:* Knowing that you have access to adequate food and shelter.
- *Safety needs:* A sense that no one around you will harm you or allow harm to come to you.
- *Love and belonging needs:* A feeling of group identity that lets you know you fit in.
- *Self-worth needs:* An expectation that good things will come to you because you deserve them.
- *Self-actualization:* You have all that you need and work on bettering the world.

Sadly, many people get stuck on the safety level. When safety is consistently compromised, it becomes a goal rather than a reality.

For those who experience historical oppression or generational trauma, safety is always compromised. When we have lived in fear of being mistreated by the world because of the color of our skin or harmed within our home due to generational trauma or family dysfunction, safety remains the goal.

When safety is the goal, our approach to love and belonging is based on fear. We carry a fear of betrayal, abandonment, or rejection from our early experiences. We begin to focus more on what's happening in our environment than what's happening inside of us. With our instincts on hyper-alert, we never connect to our intuition.

When our social-emotional needs are unmet, developing healthy relationships is difficult. We are likely to attach to others who are also stuck and stagnant instead of bonding with healthy people.

In this state of fear and unmet needs, our sense of self-worth is based on scripts that do not reflect our growth and potential. We shrink to fit into spaces too small to accommodate our pain, passion, brilliance, or dreams. And yes, I said pain. Any place that cannot accommodate your pain cannot adapt to your dreams. Any space that requires you to separate from your pain to fit in is likely not worthy of your joy when you find it.

We cannot self-actualize when our focus is on others, and we are looking for safety. Patterns of safety are often ingrained in us via the systems we grow up in. Many parents use harsh discipline and restriction, claiming these methods are to keep their children safe and then later fail to understand why their children develop low self-esteem. When you use harsh physical punishment on a child, you become their first oppressor. You teach them their body cannot be protected, and you instill shame. For a long time, we didn't know better than to spank our children. You can no longer make that claim. All related research tells us there are negative consequences to spanking your child that far outweigh any temporary behavior control. Do not pass down this tradition.

As schools increasingly implement "safety" measures, students are losing a sense of belonging. Zero tolerance leaves no room for error at a time where children make the most mistakes. News outlets have reported several stories about elementary school students being taken away from school in handcuffs. Criminalizing children obstructs self-actualization. That way of handling misbehavior is antithetical to child development - the primary purpose of elementary school.

Organizations that demand conformity in exchange for survival also rob their members of self-actualization. In this structure, group cohesiveness is prioritized, and self-actualization remains unattainable. Getting along is good, but growth is better. We support our development when we build a high tolerance for differences and risks.

We collectively forgot, or perhaps never knew, that we are born to be great, to rise above. We need to be embraced and affirmed, not just fed and sheltered. We need room to make mistakes and room for creative expression while being continuously valued. We need support for our gifts and talents even when they don't fit within the community boundaries.

Unfortunately, what we need is not what we get. Stuck in safety mode, we get thrown off track, never being allowed to show up as our most authentic, beautiful selves. Safety feels like bubble wrap around your face, suffocating. It feels like a cage, confining. It feels like a grave, buried deep. Safety is not a feel-good place for most people.

Safety can lead us into arranged marriages or highly-esteemed careers, pretending to be happy while feeling miserable. A focus on safety could just as easily hold us captive in an abusive relationship with intimate partners, organizations, or jobs. Safety often normalizes dysfunction for the sake of fitting in.

Sometimes the safety net looks like staying small and quiet when you have been a victim. This invisibility feels like a superpower saying, "If they can't see me, they can't hurt me." That logic may hold for the child who had to survive dysfunction. But, the commitment to invisibility offers little to an adult who deserves to self-actualize.

Prioritizing safety is like wearing invisible handcuffs. Safety forces us to mimic love, belonging, and self-worth instead of actually experiencing it. We manipulate or yield to society's expectations rather than define our own happiness.

Instead of normalizing dysfunction to fit in, we must come to know that the world is big enough to receive us. Your current circumstance does not represent your true value. Don't shrink, underachieve, or suppress your dreams. Realize you've been sharing your vision with the blind.

Sometimes you have to release the psychological and social-emotional connection to people, places, and time to elevate yourself. If you are stuck or underachieving, I guarantee there is a risk you have to take, an ocean you have to swim to find your shore. There's no way around it; healing requires you to let go of your safety net.

Healing requires you to become comfortable with isolation, to receive constructive criticism, and most of all, to be willing to lead instead of following. Find your way back to your dreams, your goals, your inspiration. Become your most beautiful authentic self that challenges norms, thinks outside the box, and makes the world more accessible for everyone who dares to be different.

Don't look for acceptance; look for excellence. Be so good that people want to be like you instead of you fitting in to be like everyone else. Let the world catch up to you instead of shrinking to fit into small spaces.

I know that it may be difficult to receive permission to be yourself and to be seen as an individual. Your mind may reject this notion based on your trauma, your culture, or your schooling. But your heart knows better. Check your heart for affirmation.

Then, re-ask the question, what's more important than safety? The answer is belonging, self-worth, and giving back to the world. These acts cannot be reproduced by mimicking behaviors that we think make us safe. They have to come from our most beautiful, authentic selves.

Activity Six: Make Mistakes on Purpose

Rather than spending energy trying to avoid mistakes to manage your image, practice taking risks this month. Keep a daily journal of the risks that you take. The goal is to have as many attempts at failing as you can by the end of the month. Give yourself a chance to fail at something at least once a day. Some examples are:

1) Make contact with someone who could enhance your career. Invite them to lunch or set up an online meeting to talk about your work or ask for advice.

2) Ask someone on a date that you think is out of your league but would like to get to know.

3) Invest money in crypto currency or the stock market that you can afford to risk without consequences if you lose it.

4) Try to sell someone something. You can put an item on sale with an online posting.

5) Make a statement about your belief that is different than someone else's. You don't need to defend it though.

6) Apply for a grant.

7) Set your alarm for 5:00 a.m. to begin a new morning routine that centers around you.

8) Make an attempt to get around using public transportation.

9) Look for a new job.

10) Try to break a bad habit for one day, such as smoking.

You can try any of these more than once. Notice how you feel when you don't meet your goal and when you do. But remember the goal is to take the risk no matter what the outcome is. You win every time you take the risk.

June Daily Gems

June 1

Healing patterns are not linear. We do not just get on the path and find our stride. We find the path, look around, fall down, crawl, walk, turn around, run, jump, fly, break down, get lost, and blaze new trails. Then we do it all over again in a different order. None of this necessarily determines how much we suffer on the path. Suffering is about our resistance to something on the journey that we do not want to do or believe in. Remember, we can have pain without suffering and growth without pain. The healing journey is marked by the commitment to live our best lives.

June 2

Two steps forward and one step back is a well-known pattern on the healing path. However, we can never be in the same place we were before taking that step back. We are still more conscious, resilient, and experienced than we were before. We may return to the circumstances, but we do not return to the state of mind. Once we know, we know. The rest is just practice. Commit to the practice of healing and let go of the expectation of perfection. Wherever you are on the healing path, you are enough!

June 3

We spend more energy fitting in with others than honoring our authentic selves. Pain hurts, yet we try so hard not to cry. Pain hurts, yet we make our scars invisible. Pain hurts, yet we keep trying to convince people that we are OK. Finding space for pain starts with your acceptance of it. If we don't admit it hurts, we cannot heal. Crying, asking for help, being vulnerable, and saying that you are not OK are all part of the journey. Sometimes, this is precisely where our strength lies.

June 4

Healing is about "allowing," not "fixing." There is a difference between trying to heal yourself and trying to manipulate life on your terms. The power that healing brings is self-empowerment. Do not try to determine the specific outcome of healing. Heal no matter the outcome. Ultimately, the life you create will allow you to live in your truth, and the truth will set you free.

June 5

Refusing to feel the pain does not mean you have power, and having power does not mean you are free from pain. Comfort is not an accurate measure of healing. Denial numbs pain; perfectionism covers up shame; addiction masks regret. These defenses may help you maintain family relationships, find success in your career and support your leadership, but none of them reflects healing or accurately measure personal power. Personal power is an inside job. You use personal power to maintain physical health, find time for personal growth, lift humanity, and create your peace within. Healing is a journey. Maintain awareness of where your travel takes you.

June 6

Like the circus elephant that stays in the ring with no awareness of its power and strength, we adapt to the corner we've lived in for so long. Also, like the chained elephant never introduced to its strength, you can break yourself free. Circus trainers tame elephants as babies so that when they become adults, they do not resist. Imagine a powerful elephant with the resistance of a bunny rabbit. The elephant may eat well and remain healthy in its restricted environment, but it will never behave like an elephant. All of its strength and power will be used to carry people on its back and walk through fire for entertainment purposes. When you become tired of living for others, remember that you still have the strength of the elephant. Your advantage is that you can leave the circus.

June 7

Healing will lead you to justice, but justice does not always lead you to heal. As we address the harm that was done to us, we have so many responses to consider: confronting those who've hurt us, pursuing legal justice, disclosing publicly, and living with no family contact are all healthy responses to trauma. However, none of those responses will effectively address the pain that dwells inside. Healing is most effective when we maintain consistency between internal and external responses. For example, going no contact with family could lead to a feeling of loneliness and land you in a dysfunctional partner relationship. No matter how you respond externally, healing must be focused on the internal work.

June 8

When we believe that someone else's life needs to be fixed for our lives to be better, we are co-dependent. When we take on someone else's healing plan instead of creating our own, we are co-dependent. Just because someone else may not be as far along on the healing path does not mean that we should stop healing to save them. Co-dependency will not move you forward on the healing path. Your healing must be about you, not the people you depend on.

June 9

Just because healing is a lifelong journey does not mean that living well takes a lifetime. You are doing the work, and your life is changing. You are speaking out and speaking up. You are creating safe space for yourself and honoring your inner child. You are more intentional in your responses instead of just reacting. You are learning about your needs instead of only taking care of others. The result is fewer days of depression, healthier relationships, more self-confidence, and less isolation. You are becoming the center of your own life without beating yourself up. Take a moment to recognize and honor the work you have done.

June 10

There is no magic pill for healing. But the work of healing is magical. You can transform your life. You can learn to navigate conflict in a way that honors instead of denies your humanity. You can find your voice and face your fears which will positively alter your social landscape. You can practice presence, which will lead you to a purpose beyond your wildest dreams. It's difficult work, but the payoff is priceless. So, get your hard hat and steel-toe boots and enter the construction zone.

June 11

At low points on the healing path, with the awareness of having to start our lives over as adults, resentment can easily fester. We may feel like we will never make up for lost time, that we will never live the life we were meant to live. However, if we yield to life instead of resisting our past, nothing can keep us from our greatness and our purpose. The past can no longer harm us. We don't need to run, hide, or be ashamed.

We can confront and embrace our past and then build upon it. We can let our past gift us resilience, compassion, and hope. If we trust the healing journey, it will take us exactly where we are meant to be.

June 12

Dysfunction and survival merge, making it impossible to tell one from the other. We do not notice that our vigilance for keeping our children safe makes us too strict to build trust with them. We do not realize that the isolation that keeps us safe also keeps us judgmental because we never get close enough to people to understand them. We are unaware of how we go out of our way to avoid being seen while being filled with sadness about our unmet needs. We tell ourselves that our righteous indignation makes us strong, which is our excuse to avoid looking at our dysfunction and to resist commitment to healing. Know that there is a world of peace and joy beyond survival for those who travel the healing path.

June 13

Sort through the influences of your childhood. Nitpick the values you learned about yourself and the world that you now use to fuel self-criticism. Instead of criticizing yourself all the time, take a look at the systems that raised you. Religion produces fear and tells us to put others first. Family values train us to think as a unit. School teaches us to fit in. Systems are designed for conformity, not for healing. The healing path invites us to come out of the systems and walk alone, with others who are forging their own path. Turn the tables to use the systems according to your needs instead of allowing the systems to use you for their purposes. Decide the type of person you want to be instead of trying to be what you were told to be.

June 14

What you want, and sometimes even what you work for, is not always what you get. Often, the life we have constructed without intention hinders our actions and desires. We may want better relationships, but keep clinging to the disruptive friendships we already have. There is no room for healthy people to enter a space already occupied by unhealthy people. Intentionality is more than a concept. You must set up your life on purpose to manifest that which you intend. Intentionality means being deliberate about how you use your time, who you spend it with, and what you feed your mind. The more synchronized our thoughts and actions are, the bigger our invitation for the universe to place what we desire in our lives.

June 15

Pain is the alarm that tells you where your vulnerability lies. Pain warns you to respond to external stimuli, positions you to move in a different direction. On the healing path, you alter your alarm system, moving it from external to internal. You fine-tune your internal alert system to love over fear and harmony over acceptance. We release our need for pain to direct us, become alert, attentive, and accept what we desire. Pain is not a requirement for growth or learning. You simply heal yourself out of the pattern of pain.

June 16

Being alone with your pain is OK. This is often the space where we finally come to know ourselves, love ourselves, and learn how to care for ourselves. Oddly, when we become comfortable in the space of aloneness, we realize that we are not alone at all because our expectations of others change. We find that we were looking for someone to carry us. But, when we learn how to walk on our own, people come and walk beside us.

June 17

Life scripts are given formally through institutions such as religion and education and informally by family and friends. Our state of dependence causes us to follow these scripts without questioning how they help or hurt us. The scripts always favor the power structure and make it your responsibility to please. We vary in our willingness to challenge the scripts, but most people still live pretty scripted lives. Scripts are supposed to be shortcuts so that you do not have to work so hard to figure out life. But many adults cling to the scripts that never worked for them because permission to change the script is not in the script. From now on, you get to write your life script.

June 18

Do not give up on healing because the relationship did not work out. Do not go back to using drugs and alcohol to manage depression. Do not shrink yourself to remain in relationships where you have no voice. Keep healing, even when the pain comes. Stay on the healing path even when you travel alone. You will find your strength if you allow yourself weakness. You will build your resilience if you allow failure. You will find yourself if you are willing to lose others who do not reflect your highest meaning.

June 19

When you are alone and no one is watching, speak aloud. Listen to the sound of your voice. Sing, read, say a poem, moan, cry, shout at the television. But make a sound as a peace offering to yourself. Remind yourself that you do have a voice. When you use the bathroom, do not leave without staring yourself in the eye to make contact with your soul. When you cook, taste the food before you serve it to others, not to make sure it tastes good, but as a reminder to feed yourself first in life. When you shower, feel the soap against your skin without the wash-cloth to show love to your body. Love yourself the way you've been hoping someone else will. You are worth your attention.

June 20

We must look for opportunities to grow, creating boundaries while making sure we don't box ourselves in. Ironically, boundaries don't shut us in. On the contrary, they open up spaces for us to participate in the world. Boundaries allow us to become more significant to ourselves. We say no to serving others, so we can say yes to opportunities that help ourselves. We avoid codependent relationships so that we can invite healthy ones. We stop seeking to be rescued so that we can take more considerable risks.

June 21

We not only have to heal the wounds that others created for us, but we also have to heal the wounds that we have created. Figuring out which of our injuries are self-inflicted and which are victim wounds is not easy, and prioritizing which to address is also tricky. Pay attention to your self-harming behaviors and decisions, such as ignoring health or removing boundaries to fit in.

June 22

Babies learn to walk by mastering pre-walking skills. They know how to stand and fall, stand and fall, stand and fall. Every time they stand up, they are strengthening their legs. They learn to balance themselves. They figure out how to hold onto something to practice stepping. At no point in time do they ask anyone to teach them how to walk. They walk to fit in. They walk to fulfill their desire for independence. They walk to explore the world beyond the laps of the adults who show expression by holding onto them. They walk because nature commands them to do so. When we enter the healing journey, we must know that healing is as natural as a baby learning to walk. We do not need to be taught how to heal. We just need to practice getting up each time we fall.

June 23

The transition from seeking external validation to forming internal validation may be one of the most difficult aspects of healing. But, when we pay attention to the state of the world, we can understand that the paradigm that rewards external validation is not working. Healing requires us to let go of our inherent desire to be included in that paradigm and instead realize that it keeps people unhappy. The paradigm leads people to make decisions out of fear, not love. It teaches people to direct their energy toward convincing others of their worth, inhibiting self-awareness. People who are willing to focus on healing rather than fitting in will find peace that the world may never know.

June 24

To thrive, we have come to a place on the journey where we allow ourselves to be "out of our mind." We make "crazy" choices about our lives, try nontraditional healing practices, restructure our food choices, drastically change how we use time, and learn to talk to ourselves, hear the voice within, and believe in the unseen. This change of emotions requires a shift in our responses to the world. Instead of reacting, we must initiate. Instead of resisting, we must yield. Instead of claiming the pain, we must declare our resilience. Ultimately, we heal the mind with the ageless, timeless practice of present awareness.

June 25

For every action, there is a reaction. Everything that you do causes an effect, no matter how small. When we set boundaries, people push back. When we try to change our eating habits, our body sends cravings. When we start meditating, our mind wanders. When we try to exercise, our body hurts. Taking better care of ourselves causes a strain on relationships built on dysfunction. Keep your eyes on the prize. In time, peace and joy will override the negative consequences.

June 26

If you know you are allergic to cats, you do not visit a house without asking the owner to put the cats away. If you are allergic to peanuts, you triple-check the ingredients on everything before you cook. If you cannot swim, you do not jump off of the diving board. These things can harm you. The way that you know they can hurt you is that you have likely had a bad reaction to them in the past. So, we must consider the same self-care when considering spending time with toxic people. You do not need permission to avoid people any more than a person allergic to peanut butter would need to decline a peanut butter sandwich.

June 27

When we ask for or expect from others what we are not willing to give to others or ourselves, we get in our own way. We are not charity cases. We are agents of change. If we want the universe to reflect empathy toward us, then make sure that we offer compassion to others and ourselves. We cannot both live a life of bitterness and complain about the lack of empathy we are shown. We cannot dismiss other people's pain and expect people to respect ours. No matter how much we have suffered, we are still responsible for what we offer people.

June 28

Toxic people are not mean all of the time. Part of what makes them unhealthy is the inconsistency and unpredictability of their behaviors. They are often charming and fun to be around but cannot be trusted. Toxic people are not always bossy. Sometimes we are attracted to unhealthy people because they are needy, and we want to feel needed. These relationships may feel like a perfect match. But they are a perfect storm. We must remove the poison from our internal system so that toxic people find us less attractive. The internal toxin that manifests as "I need someone to take care of," "I need someone to take care of me," or "I have no boundaries" are 'welcome' signs for toxic people. We must heal to take down these signs.

June 29

Bodily autonomy means that you have complete responsibility for what happens to and with your body. No one has a right to touch you without your consent or to force you to do things with your body by manipulation. Bodily autonomy also gives you the freedom to tell the story of your body. You can talk about what happened to your body. You can dress how you want, share yourself with whomever you want, and go where you want without permission from others. Therefore, you do not owe anyone silence about your body experience. You get to speak, or not, about your body. This decision should be boldly considered regarding your right to bodily autonomy.

June 30

We must direct our current behaviors and shape our current environment toward the better future we desire. Like quitting smoking, there is never a wrong time to heal. No matter how deep into a path of dysfunction the abuse has taken you, healing will always enhance your life. Even if we are living pretty well, conscious healing will make our lives even better. Healing matters because we become our best selves.

July

How to Heal Childhood Trauma without Forgiving the One Who Caused It

Forgiveness is an evolutionary phenomenon necessary for building and sustaining a community. Minimizing conflict preserves cooperation so that groups can achieve goals. Noticeably, people practice forgiveness more readily among loved ones and withhold forgiveness from people they have no desire to be in relationships with. Family members and people who share a loving relationship are drawn to share physical and emotional space. Forgiveness allows them to do so in the face of harm.

Forgiveness has evolutionary priorities. Misbehaved children, neglectful parents, careless spouses, and demanding grandparents are frequent beneficiaries of forgiveness. Moreover, because forgiveness is extended, children can be raised in low-conflict environments, weddings can be executed smoothly, and family reunions can be a joyful experience. This evolutionary pull toward forgiveness makes unforgiveness a radical act that could hardly be associated with healing.

Some mental health professionals and religious leaders consider forgiveness the holy grail of healing. Regardless of the depth of harm or the offender's lack of repentance, forgiveness is touted as a thera-peutic or spiritual objective. Any discomfort or negative emotions surrounding the inflicted harm are assumed to be related to a psycho-meta-spiritual bond between the offender and the survivor. "Don't let someone rent space in your head" is a familiar command given to forgive. The virtue of forgiveness has incentivized some survivors of harm to wear it as a badge of honor. "I've forgiven the person who hurt me" is sometimes a spiritual pledge or an emotional emblem.

People sometimes put forgiveness at the top of their healing agenda because it helps them fit into systems of family, culture, and religion. But support for true healing is harder to find. However, when forgiveness is extended for the wrong reason, more harm than good may be done. Forgiveness out of fear is not forgiveness. Fear of isolation, retribution, or failure is still just fear. Forced forgiveness, like pseudo-love, will often lead to disappointment.

More critical than forgiveness are the tasks of connecting to your inner child, taking care of your body, creating healthy boundaries, and letting go of secrets. Forgiveness does not override these critical aspects of healing. For several reasons, forgiveness should never be required of a person who has experienced trauma.

1) Unforgiveness does not equal hate or a desire for revenge. The word forgiveness has hundreds of synonyms in the thesaurus. However, the word "unforgiveness" isn't even in the dictionary. Therefore, when a trauma survivor states they don't forgive, erroneous assumptions usually follow. Rarely are they asked what unforgiveness means for them. Most of the survivors of childhood trauma have no desire for revenge and do not use the word 'hate' to describe their feelings. Most often, they were harmed by family members, making hate highly unlikely since hating kin is in opposition to evolutionary marking.

Unforgiveness, as clear as I can define it based on my work with thousands of survivors, is: "The conscious recognition that the person who has caused harm is no longer seen outside of the harm they caused." The only association the survivor has with the violator is the harm they once caused. Thus, the violator's full humanity may be permanently dismissed to the point where their death will bring a sense of relief. Neutrality of violator's death is not the same as hate or as hope for harm. It's based on the violator's assumed inhumanity.

2) Trauma requires a focus on self, not another person. To suggest to a survivor that their healing is contingent on resolving a relationship with the person who harmed them is a secondary harm. The suggestion can create more profound feelings of victimization. Healing requires survivors to focus on their relationship with themselves. Sometimes the forgiveness of self is required.

Forgiveness of self may be the missing connection to the inner child. As adults, survivors often feel far removed from their childhood selves for survival. Ignoring, denying, or normalizing the pain quiets the inner child for the adult to function. The psychological gymnastics between the inner child and adult psyche may have resulted in self-blame or self-neglect. If that is the case, forgiveness of self may be required, but not a forgiveness of others. As survivors heal their relationship with themselves, the forgiveness of others may or may not arise.

3) Space to experience a lack of forgiveness is often necessary for survivors to find their voice. A survivor's lack of forgiveness may be evidence that they are living in their truth and should not be interpreted as revenge. Survivors are often wrongfully blamed for disruption in their family, job, or organization, and asking survivors to remain silent is too often an indirect requirement of forgiveness.

Justified anger, depression, and anxiety are often interpreted as a need for forgiveness. However, forgiveness does not override the process of healing deep wounds. Trauma is a complex experience that is lodged within the psyche. It can affect every aspect of a person's life. While forgiveness contributes to a community's cohesiveness, the harmed individual pays a heavy price.

Forgiveness arises in hurt people when circumstances are met. But, no one can determine the conditions of forgiveness for another person. Forgiveness is a natural process, as is unforgiveness. We must trust that more critical work needs to be done when a person is in a state of unforgiveness. People who are suffering should be invited into healing spaces, not into a premature state of forgiveness.

Five Healing Practices

Five practices open survivors up to do the heart work of healing in ways that do not require forgiveness. The key is for the victim of harm to focus on themselves, not others.

#1 Live Openly

Slowly drop the secrets you carry about your past by disclosing to friends and trusted colleagues, not just your therapist. Choose good listeners who can help process your feelings instead of trying to fix you. Living openly is not about telling everyone you know but about no longer caring who knows. It is an ongoing process, not a task. Coming fully out of denial takes time. Conversations about your trauma don't have to be direct. You can use any art form to process or express your emotions.

When you have been committed to silence and begin to move away from that commitment, it doesn't always feel right. You may feel that you are the one betraying someone else, anticipating a consequence for your decision. After hiding pain instead of healing it, you may experience increased anxiety as you begin letting go of secrets. That anxiety is trying to protect you from doing something you will regret: living openly. But, your desire to live openly is not the problem. The problem is feeling responsible for protecting those who have done you harm. You are not responsible for them. They must do their own healing. When you allow yourself the freedom to choose how you live, the anxiety will lessen over time. Ultimately, healing and hiding are mutually exclusive.

#2 Let Go of Toxic Relationships

When you take forgiveness off the priority list, you may look at your relationships differently. As you allow yourself to feel the sense of betrayal you have been repressing, you may see them as toxic. They may see you as weak for not being able to "move on." Toxic people are those unreasonably demanding or insensitive to your needs. The request for silence and the requirement for you to share space with people who've harmed you are toxic expectations.

Toxic people are not always mean. Sometimes, they are manipulative or passively harmful. If you have to shrink yourself emotionally to be in the presence of someone, you are in a toxic relationship.

In a toxic relationship:

- You cannot express hurt feelings.
- You spend most of your time hiding what you feel.
- If you say anything contrary, you will be ostracized.
- Power is imbalanced. You feel powerless.

When you identify toxic people, you must distance yourself from them. Like living openly, distancing yourself from toxic people is a process. Some people cut off contact with toxic people at once, going "no contact." Other people distance themselves slowly, especially if children are attached to the toxic person. Whether immediate or over time, removing toxic people from your life must be an intentional act. Do not allow preconditioned forgiveness to get in the way of your intention.

#3 Understand the Context

Try to understand your family and cultural dynamics that make silence the rule. Don't be afraid to explore power dynamics. In what other ways does forgiveness as the denial of harm show up in your environment? How was that expectation revealed? Who made the rules? How did you know when you were safe or not? Clarifying your context can offer insights about your response to harm, and those new insights may empower you to make new choices. You may be tempted to try to understand why someone harmed you. But asking 'why' will not help you understand your trauma. The 'why' is not as important as understanding the 'how.'

How did the person have access to you? How were you unprotected? How were you given signals to remain silent? How did the harmful person present themselves to you and your family? How was power expressed in your environment? How was power earned? How were you targeted? These are the types of questions that will help you build an empowering narrative based on your reality. You empower yourself when you ask the right questions. And when you empower yourself to question and assess, creating boundaries becomes more effortless.

#4 Reconcile with the Inner Child

The boundaries you create will help you reconnect with your inner child. The inner child is the mind's remnant of the traumatic past. The subconscious holds a space that remains child-like when the psyche is wounded. It can manifest as self-sabotage or unhealthy behavior.

The measures your inner child takes to survive the trauma often appear stupid, immoral, or weak to your adult self that is actively trying to hold life together. As an adult, only you can rescue and heal your inner child and manifest love where there was judgment. The process of soothing the inner child is considered "re-parenting" your-self. However, as long as your adult mind prioritizes maintaining rela-tionships with toxic people, connecting to your inner child is unlikely. You are not re-parenting. The inner child wants to feel safe. They will respond to unsafe environments by shutting down or acting out, leading to depression and anxiety.

On your own, you can find pictures of yourself as a child and place them beside you as you write a letter to your younger self. Pick out a child at the playground who reminds you of yourself and silently state words of affirmation. Just make sure you keep a safe distance from the child. Swing on the swings while you are there if no children are present. Play and laugh out loud.

In seeking therapy, ask therapists how they incorporate inner child work into treatment. But avoid treatments that focus only on inner child work. Healing requires a lot of processing to understand the full scope of your trauma. Just getting in touch with your inner child will not suffice.

Every aspect of healing is a process. Inner child work can be over-whelming and sometimes unbearable. Don't turn it into a task. You are likely to move into and away from the work throughout your healing journey. That's perfectly fine.

#5 Go Against the Grain

You have to be willing to break some rules, exert power over your life, and then make your own rules to live your life by design. Rules are made for functionality, but not necessarily to optimize anyone's life. We are taught not to break the rules, even when the rules break us. Outdated, dysfunctional, or misguided rules often stand between you and your ability to design your optimal life.

No matter how many family members request your continued presence at the holiday gatherings, you *can* stop attending. You can also stop attending religious ceremonies and practice spirituality on your own. Stop responding to stressful phone calls, lending money upon request, and sacrificing your bodily autonomy to make others happy. Not everyone has to like or approve of your decisions. At some point, all thrivers have gone against the grain. They've had to disappoint people, challenge the status quo, and live in isolation until they found a supportive community.

The State of Unforgiving

You know how to forgive. You have done so many times in your life. You don't have to force yourself to forgive. Forgiveness and unforgiveness are natural states of being. They both arise when circumstances are met. Remember these three truths about forgiveness before you try to force yourself to forgive.

1. Every harmful act is forgivable by someone, but not necessarily by the victim who has been harmed.

2. Everyone can forgive some things, but not forgive everything.

3. Forgiveness is neither necessary nor sufficient to move along the healing journey.

Healing is a lifelong journey. Healing practices can take you much further on the journey than silence and forgiveness. At some point in your healing, forgiveness may arise or it may never arise. Set your intention on healing instead of getting along. Your focus on heart work will keep you on your lifelong healing journey. You can use your voice to tell how your pain began and how suffering ended when your healing begins with self-care.

Activity Seven: Back to the future

- 1. Find childhood pictures that correspond to the chart on the following page. Use just one image per age range for a total of four images.
- 2. Set a one-minute timer to focus on each image one at a time.
- 3. Rank the presence of each trait for the age period of focus. Use a ranking scale of 1 to 10. Ten meaning you feel highly confident that the trait was present during the age range.
- 4. After all categories are ranked, self-reflect on the people and events in your life when traits 1-8 were present versus the presence of 9-12.
- 5. Write your reflection in a poem (not a journal)

	Trait	Age 5-12	Age 12-18	Age 18-30	Age 30 +
1	Curiosity				
2	Laughter				
3	Confidence				
4	Brilliance				
5	Creativity				
6	Feeling loved				
7	Confusion				
8	Talented				
9	Sadness				
10	Fit				
11	Anger				
12	Bitterness				
13	Invisible				

July Daily Gems

July 1

Your heart may still be in a crisis from the abandonment or betrayal you experienced decades ago. Your mind is still imprisoned from trying to hold onto the love that should have been unconditional. But it wasn't. Now, one rejection feels like 1000 pricks with a needle and can leave you breathless. With your next breath, inhale love and exhale any doubt that you are lovable. You do not have to seek love. You just have to honor it within yourself.

July 2

The way to improve your life is to change patterns in your life. Change your perspectives so that you can see patterns that do not work for you. Start with an evaluation of how you spend your time. If your practice is to spend time with the familiar instead of the healthy, consider that. When you see differently, you do differently. When you do differently, your life changes.

July 3

When we experience relationships as "I can't live without you," "I live to make you happy," "You mean everything to me," or "I'm nothing without you," we fall victim to imitations of love instead of being empowered by true love. There are abandonment issues, loneliness, identity status, codependency, and a host of other emotional attachments that we call love. If you are having problems around love, clarify your definitions against your experience. Your definition should empower you rather than hold you hostage.

July 4

Making space for complexity in our lives will give us faster insight into healing. When our brain develops in an environment that does not feel safe, it creates simplicity by narrowing our experiences into smaller frames, good versus evil, happy versus sad. When we feel powerless and vulnerable, perceptions rule because very little processing can occur in survival mode. Now that we are on the healing journey, we have to learn how to process the complexities of our experiences. We can be angry about the decisions that we have to make to grow. We can feel relieved by a breakup even though we miss a relationship. We can feel everything instead of just the feelings that make sense. Feel the emotions and then process them to further your healing.

July 5

We have arrived at the healing path because the pain has directed us here. After all else failed, we came looking for something to ease the pain. We hoped for our silence to be heard. We hoped someone would see through our masks and love us for who we are. What a nice fantasy. Instead, we find advice to lean into the pain, to find our voice, and take off the mask. The healing path exposes us to a deeper level of pain. However, healing is the pain of birth rather than the pain of being buried alive in your mind. So, take deep breaths and push, knowing that the world is awaiting your beautiful arrival.

July 6

Disorganized attachment is signified by insecurity in relationships and uncertainty about closeness and intimacy. We may want closeness and intimacy, but when offered, we experience anxiety. The anxiety could be physiological or psychological. Learning to create healthy attachments is long-term work that requires a lot of mindfulness. It is essential to know what your work is and what pieces belong to the other person in your relationship. You cannot do the other person's work to sustain a relationship. You can only do your own.

July 7

Healing is not about figuring out what is wrong with us, nor is it about trying to validate ourselves. Healing is about being present with what comes up in order to become our most empowered (not perfect) self. When we accept that there is nothing wrong with us, we no longer have to defend ourselves. As long as we listen to and like ourselves, our choices are not dictated by who likes us or listens to us. We simply live in a state of learning and growing through acceptance. Make your mantra "I am enough."

July 8

The more we delay an active commitment to healing, the more loss we are likely to accumulate, even while achieving pockets of external success. We lose intuition when we avoid pain by denying our feelings. We lose our willingness to risk getting ahead out of fear we will be rejected and abandoned. We compromise our love of self to accept others. We hide instead of exploring to avoid getting hurt. We give our power away having never learned how to focus on ourselves. Heal your heart, your head, your life. Invest in your thriving.

July 9

Hard Truth to Swallow: To begin to love ourselves, we must stop calling what we give to others "love." If you claim to love others but not yourself, you are living with a distortion of love. For, you cannot give to others what you do not have. You must have "love" before you can provide it. Not loving yourself is inherent in how you have offered what you called 'love.' So, loving yourself requires relinquishing that distorted definition of love. Changing your narrative depends on redefining love accurately.

July 10

Sometimes shame is triggered without conscious thought. Most of us do not go around feeling shame. The shame may manifest as extreme shyness without awareness of the fear of being unloved if people knew about the abuse. You may become easily defensive because you perceive people as not liking you. You may avoid physical intimacy because you do not want to have a physiological response. Being conscious of our reactions and going within is how we practice self-awareness. Shame can underlie many dysfunctional patterns in our lives despite our resilience. Finding where shame hides is one discovery of healing.

July 11

Where or how do you start to heal? That is a frequent question that can be answered in many ways, yet, the healing journey is too personal to be scripted. As much as healing is about changing and growing, healing happens with understanding and intentions. Where you need to begin depends on what you need. What many people need is a clearer understanding of living authentically and with transparency. The journey can start with reading books or factual information about living with peace and authenticity. We have to understand healing beyond the desire to feel better. We must gather information beyond our personal experience.

July 12

A healthy relationship with oneself is similar to a healthy relationship with others. If you stop paying attention to your inner connection, you will suffer. Many survivors treat healing like a diet instead of a lifestyle. When we are in crisis, we put in a lot of effort to spend time with healthy people, work out, read, meditate, and use our voices. However, when the crisis is over and our lives feel balanced, we slowly stop doing the things that put our lives in balance. There is no autopilot or quick fix in healing trauma. We heal when our practices are consistent and conscious.

July 13

Action speaks louder than words. When there is a discrepancy between your thoughts and your actions, your mind must determine which to follow. When your actions have been in place for a long time, your actions will win the argument. You cannot just change your thoughts to heal. You must change your actions to heal. If you simply apply the same old actions to new ideas, then your mind will believe your actions and ignore your thoughts. Thinking you are innocent doesn't change anything when your actions represent shame. Saying that you have moved on doesn't mean you have when your actions display that you are full of pain. Thinking you deserve love doesn't mean much when your actions characterize disgrace. Your mind will likely yield to your actions, so make your actions count.

July 14

The saying goes, "the truth will set you free." That is the space where our healing lies, in the truth. No matter who refuses to believe us, the truth is the truth. Living in other people's denial silences us to the corner of despair. The people who choose violators over survivors are the more damaged victims, the more tortured souls. When we live in our truth, they can have no part of us because we reflect their denied pain. They often die trying to stay ahead of the lie. We free ourselves when we choose the truth, no matter what the consequences.

July 15

If we spend all of our emotional energy trying to find people to support us in our healing journey, we can end up feeling isolated and alone. Our lives are meant to be complete, contrary to that feeling of emptiness that we carry. We can broaden the perspective from which we live and draw people to our strengths, not just look for people who will bandage our wounds. A person who does not know how to have a conversation about pain may be a great movie companion. A friend in denial of their pain may be the best workout partner. A co-worker may help you process your frustrations around parenting. Attending events in communities that you do not belong to may help you build unique relationships. We heal when we face our issues head-on. However, much of our healing is also indirect, based on how we restructure our lives. We do not have to look for specific support. We may already have more support than we realize.

July 16

A beautiful lie may be more popular than an ugly truth. But the ability to see ourselves accurately and love ourselves gently is essential growth on the healing journey. The ability to see others accurately and love with boundaries is equally important. The truth is not always convenient, and the freedom to live in it can be costly. The healing journey requires a commitment because living a lie can be tempting when it is more convenient. Of course, the convenience is temporary.

July 17

If you do not consciously change something in your life, nothing in your life is likely to change for the better. You do not always have to make significant changes for your life to improve. Often, small changes over time yield substantial changes in the long run. One small change leads to another small change, and another until you become bold enough to take giant leaps. For so many people, the first small change that can make a big difference is acknowledging and shifting how we view relationships.

July 18

In healing, we can use our pain to find our purpose or, at least, our passion. We cannot erase past pain, but we can manifest the future with our resilience. Our healing is even larger than us, a part of shifting how the world deals with pain. Ignoring pain does not move humanity forward. Healing pain does. Ignoring pain leads to resentment, conflict, under-development, fear, and uncertainty. Healing pain leads to compassion, commitment, growth, and development. Healing creates, hiding destroys. We can make the conscious leap from hiding to healing to turn our pain into our passion.

July 19

Every morning, you wake up in the same bed. When you open your eyes first thing in the morning, all that awaits you is potential. How far into your day you get before losing sight of that day's potential depends on the decisions you made yesterday. The decisions you make today determine your potential for tomorrow. We are never powerless, and we are never without personal responsibility, no matter how much trauma we still carry.

July 20

Getting back into your body means being present and mindful in everything that you do. Reconnect with your body in purposeful ways that bring good health, pleasure, or admiration. When you disconnect for the pleasure of another, to feed negative emotions, or to punish yourself, you develop an antagonistic relationship with your body, remaining critical and perpetually disappointed with how you look and how you feel. This adversarial relationship with your body is an obstacle on the healing path. The messages there are that you are not in control of your body and that you are never enough. Neither of those things is true.

July 21

Healing is ugly, disorderly, awkward, unpredictable, and over-whelming work that sometimes produces anger, regret, fear, and uncer-tainty—at least for a while. An unwillingness to lean into the abyss of healing is understandable. It seemingly hurts more than the trauma, but only because we practiced numbing or denial for so long. Healing is a significant life change that requires a commitment to see the benefits. Do not give up.

July 22

Healing is not so much about what we can make happen as it is about what we can allow. Sometimes we get in our way by trying to *make* changes instead of *allowing* changes. Healing is a natural process. You naturally pay attention to what is happening inside of you to capitalize on your instincts. Naturally, you allow things to die that no longer serve you and give birth to something that renews your essence. Growing pains are also natural. Like toddlers learning to walk, we repeatedly fall over and bump our heads. Like the child, we seek freedom and independence and must get back up.

July 23

Instead of resisting our feelings, we lean into them to understand that we are not our feelings. Feelings are simply our messengers. They bring us information about ourselves in relation to the world. Instead of living from our feelings, we learn to explore them. We can relax even when we wake up feeling anxious about our day. We can feel at peace as we close people out of our lives. We can feel assured as we take risks to build something new. Our healing cannot always be measured by the emotions that arise on any given day.

July 24

We cannot right the wrongs that have been done to us. But we can write the wrongs that have been done to us. We can make anything "write" on our healing journey, even when we feel we have nothing left. There is a way to write that promotes healing rather than keeping us in a victim mode. The objective is to process as we write, not just state what someone did to us. We use the pen to help analyze, not just criticize. The paper is a safe place to watch the volcano erupt. As the lava spills onto the page, it singes the ropes that once bound your heart.

July 25

Scripts are handed to us before we learn to speak or read. Scripts are useful for creating shortcuts for decision-making, developing a sense of community, and predicting behaviors. Scripts are pretty useful within healthy environments. However, healing also requires us to update, revise, or throw away scripts that no longer serve us. Narratives are our interpretations within the script. We create our narratives, but when our scripts disempower us, our narratives do as well. When we operate from victim scripts, we create victim narratives. As we move through the journey, the narration of our experiences changes. We must keep this in mind and check ourselves for updates now and then.

July 26

Isolation can be an excellent tool for healing. If isolation fills you with bitterness and hopelessness, that is the path of victimization, not healing. The path of victimization and the path of healing are often confused because they can feel equally isolating and filled with painful discoveries. However, the path of victimization is a downward spiral of life out of control, while the healing path is a slow walk into peace and personal responsibility.

July 27

"Trigger" is a general term. All triggers are opportunities to move further along the healing path. Whatever comes up in a trigger is coming up to be healed, not hidden. Many triggers make us shut ourselves down or cause us to become irritable. A person may experience so many triggers that they live most of their lives shut down and irritable. They are rarely their authentic self because they constantly respond to fear, even though they may appear to be living a "normal" life. You must lean into the trigger to heal it and resist the pull to just react to it.

July 28

If you are working on changing the world but not changing yourself, you will not find peace. Your work will always feel like work, and no matter how the world changes, your heart will still feel broken. Only if you work on changing yourself will you create peace. The changes you make within will be reflected in the world. Everywhere you show up, you will bring peace into the space. When you become the change, you do not have to demand change from others. Healing does not require you to be a martyr. It requires you to be authentic. Once you internalize the work of living authentically, healing is no longer work. The work is who you are, not what you do.

July 29

You may have believed that 'good enough' is as good as it gets, but some part of you believes you can do better. The evidence is in your continual efforts to be in spaces where people are trying to heal. Begin by stating your intention to heal. Your brain may tell you to prepare for the worst to avoid disappointment. But preparing for pain does not ease the pain; it just lowers your motivation to live without it. Focus on living well. Picture exactly what *you* want, not what society tells you to have. Have some markers of success on this journey so that you are not settling for just good enough. Plan for the best possible ending.

July 30

It is easy to beat ourselves up about how far we have to go. Sometimes we need to remember how far we have come. The healing that you have done is significant, no matter where you are on the journey. You have been healing since you were a child. You have applied what you know based on what resources you have within the support system you have built. You cannot ask for more than that. Tomorrow you have a chance to do more, grow more, heal more, and look more deeply within. Today, express gratitude for how far you have come.

July 31

Update your narrative as you heal. Speak from a place of being a survivor instead of a victim. Talk more about your growth and the changes you have made. Share more of how you manage your life instead of how trauma ruined your life. Your narrative is how you dress for the world. Present yourself in clothes that fit as you lose the weight, the burden of being a victim. Updating your narrative shows that you are aware and empowered as you face the challenges of being a survivor on the lifelong healing journey.

August

Which Meditation is Right for You?

Many people have wondered if meditation would improve their lives. Among other things, meditation can be described as a healthy habit, fad, religious practice, or an escape from reality. But could meditation be right for you? The biggest challenge is getting started and finding a life-long meditation practice is a process of trial and error.

I grew up in a religious family. On Sunday mornings, my father would summon all seven of us children to his and my mother's bedroom. We would kneel around their king-sized bed for prayer that lasted longer than my first-period class in high school. I was taught to pray and how to pray. I always started with giving thanks to the Almighty God for waking me up in my right mind. That was presumptuous, but I followed orders. I prayed a lot as a child and as an adult. I reaped the benefits that research suggests I would.

As I got further detached from religion for several reasons, my prayers began to change. Ultimately, I came to understand God as an extension of my spirit. I wanted to connect to God, not just worship and plead to God. If prayer was an opportunity to talk to God, meditation was an opportunity to listen. I stopped asking for what I knew God had already given me and stopped offering thanks to God for taking care of me. I don't expect my child to walk into my room every morning and thank me for feeding them the day before. My care is a given. The way my children live their lives is plenty of thanks. I wanted to understand more about God's expectations of how I should live my life. For that, I needed time to listen to God, to define my connection to God. I found that easier to do once I stopped giving that responsibility over to the clergy. I began to practice meditation as stillness, a time for me to shut up and listen to God, to myself.

The benefits of meditation depend on your purpose. Not everyone who practices meditation is looking for God. Meditation can still quiet the mind and reduce anxiety. News sources report that some elementary schools have implemented meditation as a replacement for detention and other schools have added it into their normal day. In an overstimulated world where something is always vying for our attention, an invitation to get quiet is a necessary experience.

Perception occurs on three basic levels to help us navigate through life. The first level is physiological experience. We feel pain and we respond. There is not much thought involved at all. We blink if something comes close to our eyes. Discomfort triggers us to respond without thought. It doesn't matter if the discomfort is external or internal. The second level of perception is thought. Incoming stimuli is filtered through the mind. Our reactions are based on what we decide is most beneficial. Unfortunately, thoughts are limited to the experience and knowledge of the thinker. If the thinker is operating from fear, the thoughts will be guided by fear rather than best interest. The third level of perception is consciousness beyond the mind. It works by being present enough to hear what is not said, see what is not shown and feel what cannot be understood with the thinking mind. This level of perception comes only with quieting the mind with the use of silence.

Reading a thousand books will not yield the highest level of understanding. One hundred therapy sessions will likely not teach you to hear the sound of your heart. Meditation is the practice that you must enter into. You don't need formal meditation. You just need to create silence in each day. There are answers within the silence. There is information that comes through silence. Continued growth and development comes in the language of silence.

Over the years, I have run into many obstacles in trying to maintain a regular meditation practice. I have yet to be as consistent as I would like, but I am fairly consistent. I am a witness to its benefits. There are five elements for consideration if you have an interest in exploring how meditation can improve your healing journey: position, duration, focus, sound, and time.

Position

Prayer position is relatively easy. Tradition is that you find your way to your knees. I don't know anyone who meditates hunched over a bed on their knees. Positions in meditation typically signify an open heart, so, the chest is visible.

Finding a comfortable meditation position is critical for sustaining a practice. Meditation positions often have some combination of bent knees and a straight back. You have to find a position that your body will eventually adjust to. Depending on your body flexibility and wellness, you may prefer to sit in a chair.

You don't have to punish your body to meditate. You may feel initial discomfort, but you should not feel pain. Find a position that feels open. Nontraditional options also include walking and lying down.

If you need to move around to avoid harming yourself from remaining in discomfort for too long, do so. The goal is to find your comfortable position, not to force one that eventually motivates you to quit.

Duration

Sitting in silence for meditation slows down our perception of time. You may set yourself up to fail if you start with an ambitious goal like meditating for an hour. Meditation practice can be as short as five minutes. How long one should meditate depends on the purpose of their practice. If a person uses meditation for something specific, such as a cure for depression, quitting smoking, or incentive for creativity, significant time may be required. If meditation is used for self-reflection or grounding, one may need less time.

Meditation can be practiced daily or sporadically. More time does not always equal more results. If meditation becomes a habit that you engage without an appreciation for its value, you compromise its effectiveness. You want to make sure you practice meditation, not just practice the practice of meditation.

Focus

Meditation practices can focus on heightening mental awareness or connecting to your body. In body-focused meditations, you may be directed to start by scanning your body. You're invited to pay attention to your breathing and each body part. Here, you find your way inward by connecting to each part of your body. Some guides aim for total concentration on breathing. Other meditations guide your mind to a specific place, focusing on the experience in order to let go of all external stimuli. You may be led step-by-step through a memory or to an imagined place. The goal is to allow yourself to experience everything in your mind without judgment.

Chakras, a group of seven points in the body that make up our energy system, are also a focus of meditation. Balancing them creates physical and psychological wellness. Chakra meditations focus on removing energy blockages from our system.

Sound

Sound is an essential aspect of meditation. Some people prefer to meditate in complete silence. Some require ambient sound to aid them in traveling inward. Others prefer guided meditation, following someone's voice.

The ambient sound should be relaxing. However, relaxing is subjective and requires trial and error. Some people prefer a particular instrument such as a piano or saxophone. Other meditation sounds capture nature, such as the ocean, rain, or wind. You may change the sounds with each meditation, or you may stick with a favorite. Meditation becomes practice when you find what works for you.

Time

Meditation in the morning may feel different than at night. You are not limited to attaching meditation to waking up and going to bed. Some group meditation sessions occur in the middle of the day. The time that you are willing to meditate is the best time to do it.

Formality in meditation should offer guidance, not rules. Whether you participate in a group practice or sit alone, the point is to engage without judgment. Judgment means your mind is still trying to lead. Meditation is intended to quiet your mind. So, however you engage, engage with ease.

Meditation is a unique experience no matter how many people you share your practice with or how similar your reasons are for doing it. There is no wrong way to meditate. Meditation is a tool. It can help increase creativity and improve cognitive processes as well. It declutters the mind so that you can live more authentically. It doesn't compete with prayer; it complements it. It doesn't override logic; it balances it. But, each person must find their unique meditation practice.

Activity Eight: Meditation

For the next 31 days, utilize the daily gems to begin a 5 minute or longer meditation practice.

1) When you awake in the morning, read the daily gem. You don't have to stick to the one specified for the day. Choose any one. You can even use the same gem for all 31 days.

2) Do the reading first thing in the morning, before you do anything for someone else. Don't get dressed for work, feed anyone, or take any calls before you read.

3) If you typically start your day by reading a holy book, read it after you read the daily gem. The point is to do something different for 31 days.

4) After you read your daily gem, find a comfortable space to meditate. Set your phone timer to 5 minutes. As you become comfortable, increase the time. See if you can increase your time to 20 minutes by the end of the month.

5) You choose the sound and focus for your meditation. You can experiment with different choices throughout the month.

6) Observe the changes that take place over the month. Your body may feel more energetic, your mind may feel more at ease, or your

motivation may be increased. Just observe with expectation for 31 days.

7) The end of the month is the right time to decide if you want to continue the practice or try something else. But, continue to invite change into your life.

August Daily Gems

August 1

The emotional labor of healing can leave us feeling quite vulnerable. No matter how far we go to make ourselves appear 'normal,' the insecurity of not feeling normal remains. No matter the lengths we go through to feel accepted, the fear of rejection lingers. Do not assume that anyone is doing you a favor by being with you. Do not surmise that the other person is a prize. Always participate in relationships on equal footing. It is not how the other person responds to you but how you interact in the relationship that reflects your self-value. Relax and let people see how wonderful you are. Show people how to love you by showing them how you love yourself.

August 2

We do not always know whether we are holding onto the pain or the pain is holding onto us. Sometimes when we lose someone or something precious, we hold onto the pain to validate our loss. The idea of moving beyond our pain may leave us wondering how to express or address what went wrong. However, permitting ourselves to heal the pain does not negate our past or let anyone off the hook.

154

Healing simply allows us to reclaim our lives, creating a destiny from a place of peace instead of pain.

August 3

When fear runs your life, you are likely to respond with resistance. When anger runs your life, you are likely to produce conflict. When self-pity runs your life, you are likely not to respond at all. Fear, anger, and even pity are part of a healthy lifestyle, but healthy decisions are not made from that space. You can and should acknowledge and experience the full spectrum of emotions. But, you have to accept their limitations. Emotions don't heal; they only show you what needs to be healed.

August 4

If we were raised in a dysfunctional family environment, we might have been required to develop endurance and thick skin. You may have learned as a child to commit to sticking things out to survive. This pattern of tolerance followed you into adulthood. Instead of using pain as a signal to evaluate and change direction, you may use pain as a signal to try harder. Try harder to please someone. Try harder to control your children. Try harder to be a good friend. Try harder to be successful at a job that you hate. You remain in the survival mode that you picked up as a child. Your high tolerance for pain keeps you committed to dysfunctional experiences and relationships that recycle pain from the past. Sometimes, the only way out of this cycle is time in isolation to learn what peace feels like. Sometimes you have to be willing to let go of everything to learn how to hold onto anything.

August 5

When we say, healing is difficult, we are often referring to the unfamiliarity of our next step. We usually mean that we do not know how to do something. But lack of knowledge about 'how' to do something is not the same as something being difficult to do. Healing involves learning how to narrate what we are experiencing. The words we use can influence how we experience the journey. "This is difficult" is a definitive statement. There is nothing to be done after that statement is made. However, if you can find other ways to talk more openly about the journey, solutions will come. The next step can arise from self-reflection.

August 6

This is your healing journey, for better or for worse. Healing is all about choices. We usually have to learn how to make new ones, and we sometimes have to learn how to watch and accept the consequences of our past choices. Doctors, therapists, family, clergy, friends, and other listeners can all advise on our lives, but we must ultimately take responsibility for the choices we make. So, if you yield your choice of lifestyle to someone, know that you have made a 'choice' about your preferences. It is a choice to relinquish your choice, but your responsibility for your life cannot be relinquished. Approach your ability to choose with grave seriousness.

August 7

When the world tells survivors not to cry, we must give ourselves permission to cry. When the world tells us to act like an adult now, we should honor our inner child. When the world tells us to shut up to avoid shame, we should break the silence to show strength. When the world tells us to put the abuse behind us, we have to give ourselves permission to be present in its pain. When the world tells us that we need to forgive our violators, we should forgive ourselves. Forgive ourselves for having taken the world's bad advice for so long. Let the healing begin.

August 8

You cannot change what you cannot see. Every time you run away from your pain, deny your past or resist what hurts, you lose the opportunity to see clearly. What we do not see clearly will take longer to unfold. If we want to set ourselves free, we must know the truth. With truth can come pain, regret, and despair. Truth can beat us over the head and sock us in the eye to wake us up to becoming alive. Truth never promises to be kind or gentle, just liberating.

August 9

We are driven by our perceptions of ourselves, others, and the world. Our perceptions determine our power to create peace, interact positively with others, and change the world. Your belief in your ability to compose your inner world and successfully navigate the external world matters. Notice the choice of the words 'navigate' and 'compose' as opposed to 'control.' We cannot control our healing by bullying ourselves or others with negative judgments.

August 10

There is so much beauty in healing even though it feels difficult at times. It's like watching flowers bloom in the garden, or the tides roll into the shore, or the airplane soar through the sky or the sunset on a warm summer night. It just feels good to the core as you realize that you are connected to greatness in a way that makes you powerful, not weak. When you really understand that you are enough you finally stop seeking. Then you can just soak in all the everyday moments of affirmation. Every smile that is exchanged with strangers, the kind words people say when you aren't even in the room, every time your body says yes to receive pleasure through exercise, intimacy, or meditation, and every time we accomplish a difficult task, we are reminded that healing is worth it. Every sunrise is an invitation to heal a little bit more.

August 11

As the great Eckhart Tolle teaches, "Relationships do not cause pain. They bring out the pain that is already within us." There is a way out of being stuck in a cycle of failed relationships. The way out is to go within. Begin to figure out your patterns of giving away power, then go deeper and figure out where those patterns come from. This begins the process of restoration.

August 12

So much of life is out of our control. Yet, we continue to spend our energy trying to control things that we cannot. At the same time, we ignore what we can control. When we were children, we responded to our lack of control by regulating our internal environment. We built resilience this way. As we age, we often overcompensate for our lack of control as children, attempting to control our external world instead of regulating our internal space. Resilience is necessary for surviving but is insufficient for thriving. Resilience means that we will keep getting up, no matter how many times we are knocked down. We will survive. However, thriving comes when we learn how to stop getting knocked down. We thrive when we learn to control what comes into our lives by controlling our inner lives, not the other way around.

August 13

Healthy people do not require all of your time or energy to make the relationship work, and they certainly do not require you to shrink. They will reject invitations to act as a "savior" for you. Only unhealthy people will portray themselves as the answer to all of your problems with promises to be your everything. So, when we stop looking for a hero, we will be more likely to attract healthy people.

August 14

Anger gives us a voice. But, misplaced or prolonged anger is toxic. After a while, we do not even recognize our rage and mislabel it as our personality. When anger becomes who we are instead of one of many options with which to respond to the world, we get stuck in victim mode. The very mode we are trying to get out of. Observe the use of anger in your life and see how often it doesn't get you what you want.

August 15

Disconnecting from our sexual selves does not make us safer in the world. When we disconnect at this basic level of existence behind closed doors, then what we do in the world may reflect that disconnection. Healing our sexual selves is often an important part of healing that gets ignored. But you do not get to pass on this responsibility. Healing our sexual selves prepares us to make direct demands in the world, not just toward an individual, unapologetically.

August 16

Healing leads us away from the people and places we that have become the cornerstone of our lives, and we feel lonely. The aloneness of the journey keeps so many survivors stuck in victim mode. The image of healing that we pursue doesn't match the harsh reality that healing sucks for years before it becomes "natural." But, we don't get to the good stuff if we don't work through the icky part of aloneness.

August 17

Empowerment starts with high-quality care as children. Unfortunately, there is no amount of love or care that anyone can offer you to make up for the lack of care you received as a child. You have the right and the responsibility to heal that loss, not replace it. Speak the truth that you could not speak as a child. Cry the tears that you could not cry when you were a child. Feel the pain you did not know you had a right to feel. There is so much within you that needs to be healed. No one can take away your need to be healed, and you are capable of healing no matter what your past has been.

August 18

Your brain requires information to stop repeating the outdated messages and patterns of behavior. The information you should know about your brain includes the effects of medication on depression, natural ways to improve your thinking and mood, the best food choices for the brain, and the effect of childhood trauma on the brain. The internet allows access to all these topics on video, in research articles, and on websites. Knowledge is power, and the most powerful exchange of knowledge is at your fingertips.

August 19

Going within is like going in the caves to find the treasure. If you only look right near the surface, you will not find the most valuable treasures. You have to go into the cave of your mind and get sweaty and dirty and stinky as you get deeper and deeper. It may get darker and darker and more difficult to breathe. But you have to go in far enough if you want to get to the treasure of peace. Dig deep to find the beauty of you, because what you think the violator took from you is not possible to be taken. It just got buried.

August 20

Although we cannot see what our mind is doing with our eyes, we can make assumptions about our mind's wellness based on mental performance. No matter how well your performance may be in the world, you can pay attention to your mental health if you have difficulty in the following areas. Significant wellness traits include mental flexibility, a focus on the present, cognitive predictability, emotional independence, and truthful living.

August 21

The mind can go haywire easily and frequently. Negative thoughts, feeling of loneliness, anger, or sadness can show up randomly. When these states of mind occur, it is good to know how to self-soothe. Many activities can calm the mind. Have meditation music on your mobile phone and keep a book of affirmations to start. It takes trial and error. So keep practicing until soothing becomes a way of being, and your general state of mind is a sense of peace.

August 22

Trust that you are exactly where you are meant to be on the healing journey. You are not the same place on the journey as you were last year. You will not be here this time next year. But while you are here, embrace where you are and value the uniqueness of your journey.

August 23

We cannot heal by imitation. The healing process is unique to us all despite all that we have in common. The betrayal may be similar, the pain familiar, the shame common and the fear mutual among us. But we vary in areas of strengths and weaknesses, resources and support, beliefs and awareness, situations and circumstances. Imitating what we see will not put us where someone else is on the path. We must go within to customize our path.

August 24

How many times you have failed is not important. Returning to old patterns that you know are self-destructive does not make you a failure. Even if you are stopped by fear, you are still on the healing path. Avoiding mistakes is not what makes us the great travelers on the path. What matters is your determination to get up and move forward from wherever you are today. Today is an opportunity for you to be better than you were yesterday. Do not waste it on regret.

August 25

Our society is not well, in part, because we have spent centuries directing people to resources outside of themselves. Yet, we blame people for not taking personal responsibility. Healing by going within could be the new trend if *we* set it. We do not need to try to fit in, for we were meant to lead. We have followed in silence long enough, and that has never worked for us. Are you ready to be a part of setting the trend instead of fitting in? The world is waiting for us to reveal our resilience. Let's bring evolution to the revolution.

August 26

Unfortunately, when we use relationships as evidence of our value, whether it is with children, parents, spouses, partners, or friends, we devalue ourselves. We cannot give ourselves to others in the hope of receiving love. Instead, we can learn to share ourselves with others from a place of self-love. That way, if people leave, they will not take our self-esteem with them. They will not take our value with them. We may grieve the loss of their love, but we will not have to mourn the loss of our love for ourselves.

August 27

Sleep does not come easy to those with deep emotional pain. Between insomnia, having nightmares, and the fear of the dark, we often sleep watching TV. Sleep is essential to good health, and one of the benefits of healing is to improve the quality of your sleep. Lack of sleep can contribute to medical problems, depression, and lack of mental clarity. Holistic healing requires us to treat the symptoms *and* the cause of our pain. Sleep better to heal better and heal better to sleep better. Don't just live with dysfunction.

August 28

If we had only bad memories of the family who hurt us, letting them go or putting distance between them and us would be easy. But the truth is that we give up a lot of good times and social benefits when we finally choose ourselves over family. So, leaving feels lonely, mean-spirited, selfish, and even unnecessary. But each time you are in that family environment you must pretend like you were never hurt because no one in that environment will allow you to speak. Silence is the cost of their love. It is not unconditional. You are trying to extend unconditional love to people who cannot extend it in return. The condition for their love is your silence. So, you have to choose to heal or choose to love (others), knowing that your love is not authentically you. When you choose to heal, you choose to love yourself authentically.

August 29

The energy we spend trying to get people to like us distracts us from our boundaries. Often, by the time we realize that the person has crossed our comfort and safety boundaries, we have committed to something we didn't want. When we let go of the fears of not being accepted and of being alone, we become our best advocates. We set and maintain safe boundaries.

August 30

We have a responsibility not to shrink to fit in and to spread our wings to break through barriers. Instead of living our lives in the corner, we have to be willing to come out of the corner and get a good look at our environment. The view from the middle of the room is quite different.

August 31

If you have the imagination to wonder how your life would be different if XYZ, you have the resilience to create experiences that offset the effects of XYZ. Of course, nothing can take away your experience. But we can neutralize our responses to our experiences, at least enough to build peace, joy, happiness. We can learn to trust without eroding boundaries. We can learn to risk without being paralyzed by the fear of failure. We can learn to love without tripping over fear of abandonment. We can do more than just imagine a better life. We can work toward it.

September

How to Get Off the Relationship Roller Coaster

The chaos of life leaves us hungry to connect and thirsty for someone to hold onto. Over-exposure to other people's success can trigger a craving to be significant. So, we give relationships all we've got, only to be met with disappointment before long. Your heart is still in crisis from the abandonment or betrayal of decades past. Your mind is still imprisoned from trying to capture the 'love' that the world claims is 'unconditional.' So, you look for someone to make you feel a certain way.

Unfortunately, your expectations will not be met when you enter relationships in seeking mode with a hidden agenda. This way of engaging relationships keeps you from investing in who the person is and what they have to offer because you don't see them, you only *feel* them.

Good feelings are easy to create in new relationships. Being the center of attention, getting exposed to new activities, and sharing details of your life with someone who listens will draw any two people together. You believe you are paying attention to the other person, but you are only paying attention to how that person is making you feel. You rely on the person for an inner sense of significance.

From that point on, your behaviors in the relationship become unconsciously manipulative. You may create conflict with the person, so their decision to remain with you feeds your need for significance. Conflict is a state of arousal that some couples substitute for intimacy. Becoming passive in the relationship so that the person is not tempted to leave is also manipulation. Sometimes helplessness or neediness is used to guilt the person into remaining. Each of these patterns of manipulation is based on fear and produces unhealthy relationships.

Unhealthy relationships require one or both partners to live small. Unhealthy attachment is signified by insecurity and uncertainty in relationships. There is a desire for constant affirmation. While you may get plenty of it in the beginning, relationships settle, and instead of trust and safety forming, fear of abandonment grows.

If you have unhealed trauma, a single rejection feels like death by 1000 cuts, leaving you gasping for air. Emotional or physical space can fill with doubts about your worthiness. That initial feeling of significance turns into a sense of insignificance. You swear not to let this happen again, but it does. It's not that everyone you meet is unhealthy. It's that the people drawn to neediness are unhealthy. Healthy people want to can engage from a place of love, not fear. Healing is essential if you want healthy people to gravitate toward you.

Your relationship with yourself has to take priority over your relationship with others. Try healing your own heart to capture the heart of others. Trauma is not a trait of compatibility. Working on your mental growth and development is the best way to curate friendships. However, trauma from childhood, adult broken hearts, and mental health challenges may require therapeutic exploration before healthy relationships can be established.

Self-exploration can occur through a formal therapeutic relationship, informal exploration through self-help groups, or your personal use of resources. The goal is to move away from being defined by your relationships and truly get to know who you are. Whether you seek professional help or not, understanding the basic components of self-exploration is important (see below.)

- *Evaluate your beliefs:* Knowing your beliefs does not require emotional depth. Dig deeper to know where your beliefs come from and how they serve you. Sometimes, holding onto beliefs about yourself, others or the world can infringe upon meaningful relationships.

• *Understand your worth:* No matter how much rejection you have experienced in the past, you are worthy of love. Relationships do not give you worth; they reflect your understanding of your worth. If you seek your value in relationships, you will always be an underdog and eventually disappointed.

• *Own your feelings:* Explore your feelings; don't accept them as absolute truth. Feelings are the antennas that connect our outer and inner worlds. They should teach us as much about ourselves as they do about the world. Accepting responsibility for our feelings prevents us from making others responsible for our happiness.

Self-awareness fosters transparency and authenticity with others. When you fill your life with 'you,' people have a much smaller space to fill. They don't have to be responsible for rescuing your emotions. Consider how you meet people when you are trying to build long-term friendships. Relationships that develop out of distress often dissolve once the distress is relieved. Distress includes people who are:

• experiencing grief
• having marital problems
• dealing with childhood trauma
• experiencing unemployment

When you meet people in distress, go slow. Resist trying to rescue them from their emotional pain. Support them by allowing them space to walk out of your life without judgment if their needs change. Avoid bonding over the trauma. Try to meet people at festive events or organizations. You will have a better chance of building good relationships when you meet on favorable ground. Volunteering in nonprofit organizations or serving on boards is a great way to meet people. Make a point to meet new people on an ongoing basis to avoid clinging to one person.

Not everyone will be your close friend. You must not over-rely on friends you become close to. Don't burden your close friends with the expectation to be by your side for everything. Social acquaintances can network with you, support your career endeavors, and share social events. Heavy expectations often send healthy people running in the other direction. They come into your life to enhance their sphere of influence and personal growth. Healthy people are not showing up to take up all the space in your life.

Healthy people want to know that you have other healthy friendships. They do not want to be your only friend. Long-lasting friends share their networks. You need to have something to bring to the table.

Healthy people do not want to be friends with people who surround themselves with unhealthy individuals. Unhealthy people include those who are:

- overly critical
- unmotivated
- abusers of any kind
- involved in criminal activity

Choose your close friends wisely, not based on convenience. Healthy relationships do more than prevent you from being lonely. Building quality friendships takes time. Be intentional:

- Avoid contacting new friends every day. Busy people may only be available once a month. Respect their time.
- Reach out. Don't always wait for people to contact you. Reaching out at least once a month to someone you want to develop a long-term relationship with is reasonable.
- Create interesting dialogue. Talk about the world and community happenings. Don't just talk about yourself. Show people that you are well-rounded.
- Demonstrate boundaries when necessary. Friends accept no for an answer. You don't want long-term relationships with people who are demanding. You will lose too much power in those relationships.
- Be trustworthy and dependable. Respect the effort that others put into the relationship by maintaining confidentiality when expected. Another way to be trustworthy is to be on time. You won't build relationships with patterns of no-shows and tardiness.
- Help people solve problems without being intrusive. Offer information, volunteer your time. Partner with friends on their projects. Just make sure you are assisting, not rescuing.

- Celebrate friends' accomplishments. You don't have to go out of your way. But make sure you let friends know you are happy for them. Send them a text or make a phone call. Don't rely on social media to build long-term relationships.

- Be a person that friends can be proud of. Be involved in your community, advance your career, focus on your education or have a hobby. Build an exciting life. Personal growth is contagious. Just remember to be humble as well.

- Extend invitations: Invite people to exciting events, not just places where you regularly go, such as church. Seeing a movie or play together will create good conversation. Avoid expensive propositions unless you are certain the person can afford the cost.

Even long-term relationships don't last forever. Some last for years, some last for decades. People grow apart for many reasons. Let them do so without resentment. You are not at the mercy of friendship. Both people should be there by choice, not as a captive. Leave and let go as necessary. No matter how many times people disappoint you, work on yourself to cultivate long-term relationships. If you convince yourself that good friends or good partners don't exist for you, stop and do the work to make yourself healthy enough to attract them. Keep an open mind and an open heart that attracts like-minded individuals. You will know you have found the perfect relationship balance when your mind is absent of anxiety and worry, and your heart feels connected and at peace.

Making friends is easy at any age if you consider all regular, positive interactions with people as friendship. However, developing long-term nurturing relationships with people takes more than seeing each other at social events. More meaningful friendships have characteristics that are built upon with intention. Two people share an emotional space that accommodates intimate behaviors between them. For example, they may:

• Share one-on-one time
• Visit each other's homes
• Give each other a hand
• Share in special occasions

- Call on each other to help problem-solve
- Console each other in times of grief
- Speak well of one another

Friendship is reciprocal, though it is not always fifty-fifty. Sometimes one person may have needs that consume the relationship for a while. One person may have more time to invest in the relationship than the other. Also, each person may be better at fostering some characteristics of friendship more than others.

Building healthy friendships is a skill that can be learned. Moving beyond social acquaintances comes naturally for some people. Others have to move into relationships with more consciousness to keep it from falling apart too quickly. Nevertheless, anyone can learn to develop healthy relationships. If your life is void of long-lasting friendships, you may benefit from a deeper understanding of relationships. A change in your ideas and efforts can create space for kind and generous people to come into your life and share your love.

Activity Nine: Expectations

Score the following statements from one to 5. Five means you are unwavering in these ideal behaviors.

- 1. _____ You spend quality time with yourself.
- 2. _____ You have made deliberate attempts to heal past
- wounds, such as counseling, books, etc....
- 3. _____ You are slow to criticize yourself.
- 4. _____ You keep promises you make to yourself.
- 5. _____ You tell yourself you are an attractive person.
- 6. _____ You ask for help when you need it.
- 7. _____ When you make a mistake, you readily forgive yourself.
- 8. _____ You look at yourself in the mirror other than for grooming purposes.
- 9. _____ You avoid comparing yourself to others.
- 10. _____ You love yourself more than others.
- 11. _____ You expect friends or partners to empathize with your past wounds.
- 12. _____ You require high-quality time with your partner.
- 13. _____ You expect friends to listen without judgment.

- 14. _____ You expect your people to keep promises they make to you.
- 15. _____ You expect your partner to compliment you on your looks.
- 16. _____ You want to have a voice in your relationships.
- 17. _____ You want your value in a relationship to be acknowledged.
- 18. _____ You want friends who won't let you down.
- 19. _____ You want relationships where you don't have to be perfect.
- 20. _____ You want a partner who puts you first.

Add your scores for items 1 - 10 only.
Place number here _____.

Add your scores for items 11 - 20 only.
Place the number here _____.

Consider the difference in scores; the first set of items represent how you treat yourself. The second set represent how you desire others to treat you.

If your total for items 1 – 10 is lower than your total for items 11 – 20, you expect people to treat you better than you treat yourself. When that is the case, building healthy relationships is difficult. Work on increasing your score on the 1 – 10 items.

September Daily Gems

September 1

When you see that your efforts are much greater than the outcomes, give yourself a soft landing. Do not take on an attitude of defeat. When people leave because you grow too big for the space they are used to offering you, give yourself a soft landing. Do not assume you are unlovable. When your nightmares are bigger than your dreams, create a soft landing. Your inner child has had enough criticism and absorbed enough doubt to last a lifetime. So, give yourself a soft landing, keeping your inner child from getting more scrapes and bruises.

September 2

To move forward, process your triggers for the message they bring. If your goal is to always avoid triggers, then don't answer your phone, check your email, or talk to anyone while you are away from home. But, know that you will miss important information. Triggers are not bad. They arise to alert you to delete or heal something in your life. Some triggers call us to go deeper and find out what is causing the pain. Some triggers bring back important memories to process the truth rather than the story that our mind held onto for survival. No matter how subtle or how traumatic, triggers are connected to our inner knowing.

September 3

Healing is a way of life. It never ends. We may no longer be triggered, but we are not healed. We must still watch our patterns to live from a place of love instead of fear. There are layers and layers and layers of work to be done. We will periodically have to assess how we get in our own way. Make sure that your patterns of behavior are consistent with your intended growth.

September 4

Strength is developmental. It accumulates with time, action, and intent. Resistance is spontaneous and triggered by pain. As we find our power, we lose our need for resistance. We lean into discomfort to awaken instead of resisting and living in denial. We don't develop the strength to stop an attack but rather to allow peace to flow.

September 5

Every day, we can choose to focus on our resilience and build our next step from there. Every insight that we get should be used as a tool to move forward, not as a weapon to beat ourselves with. When we notice the ways we have been sabotaging our healing, we do not have to call ourselves stupid or feel bad. Instead, we can praise ourselves for gaining greater insight. Then we can gently move out of the situation. We can learn to move forward without punishing ourselves. We are resilient, and we are enough.

September 6

Sometimes healing is not about finding the answers and certainly not about giving them. Instead, invest time in finding the right questions. The right question often does not require an answer. Awareness will arise, and through awareness, change happens. Make your questions complex enough to lead you inward with a sense of responsibility. How am I getting in my own way? What am I not seeing? Am I committed to change or committed to my story? Where have I given up personal power? How could I shift my story of victimization to feel more empowered? No matter how you respond, awareness presents an opportunity for growth.

September 7

Watch your reactions to situations that cause you strong emotions, whether the feeling is positive or negative. Do you get super excited because someone invited you to a program, the same as you do when someone buys you a gift for your birthday? If so, your brain may be receiving "attention" as important without considering the cost of how you get the attention. If your brain is not making appropriate distinctions, it may create conflict to seek attention instead of waiting for an invitation. So, pay attention to all of your strong reactions. Practice making meaning of them and remember, this takes time to develop.

September 8

Healing is about you. Heal because you deserve a good life. When your (internal) life is good, those you invite in will share in your goodness. When we change for someone else, our relationship with them along with other areas of our lives tends to suffer because our focus is not in the right place. Healing for others leads you to expect something in return that you'll never get. There is no greater return than the love you give to yourself.

September 9

Sometimes, we invest so much into our secrets and lies that letting them go seems impossible. For example, we come to believe that secrets and lies keep us safe. The logic goes, being unknown leads to being unseen, and being unseen means that people cannot hurt you. This is not true, but when we have invested so heavily in keeping our secrets and maintaining our lies, it can feel terrifying to acknowledge they're not keeping us safe after all. You must take a leap of faith to jump out of the cycle.

September 10

A life of service is a personal commitment to relieving pain wherever you stand. Even the smallest gesture of kindness you offer to someone matters. The smile you share with a stranger, the amount of money you tip, the door you hold open, the meter you feed for an unknown car is a service to humanity. The kind words you share at your job instead of complaining, the problems you solve without bragging, the compassion you show to the beggars without judgment can feed your own heart. We do not have to focus on trauma. We do not have to write a book. We do not have to tell the world about our trauma to be of service. We can transmute our pain into a practice of kindness.

September 11

We have to keep an eye on the intersections in our lives. When we change something for good, the ripple effects may not all be good. Watching the tide roll in will help you address unintended consequences. Maybe you started eating better, but now you are spending less time with significant people in your life because you no longer share meals. So, you are more isolated. Maybe you got a new job, but now you don't have time to work out. So, depression sets in. For every action, there is a reaction, and sometimes consequences are unintended. Be watchful of all the shifts happening around you, even when you are happy.

September 12

Understanding the difference between pain and suffering is essential in healing. Pain can be good or bad, but suffering always feels bad. You can have pain after working out as your muscles recover. But, if you understand that the pain came from a choice you made to improve yourself, you do not have to suffer. If you experience the same degree of physical discomfort due to an illness, you may suffer as you worry about why you are ill and if you will get better. We suffer when we focus on what we cann*ot* control. When healing is directed internally and we focus on what we *can* control, the pain does not have to lead to suffering.

September 13

Pain directs us to the problem. A person who is numb to pain is more vulnerable to death. For example, people who have diabetes sometimes end up in the emergency room because of an untreated injury. The injury was not treated because the part of the body where the injury took place was numb. The body was unable to send the alert signal of pain. When we bump into something or fall, our body sends pain signals, so you know where to direct attention. Well, the mind does that too. Pain is the alert system asking you to pay attention to something. The pain remains until we address the wound. Too often, we run away from, resist, or deny the pain instead of paying attention. When we learn to read our pain signals, we can lean in and address what is necessary to regain control of our lives.

September 14

We attract people who are sensitive to our journey when we open our hearts to be sensitive to others' journeys. We learn to walk away from toxic people when we become healthy. We create healthy boundaries when we let go of the stifling expectations of others. For every change we believe needs to happen outside of us, development first needs to occur within us. Loving ourselves is not the belief that we are flawless but the acceptance of our flaws while we work on them.

September 15

Trauma compromises the immune system. People in psychological pain have reported many illnesses, including those related to digestion, breathing, and immune strength. With that in mind, it is important to pay attention to your body and become a champion of your wellness. As we alter our life patterns for the good, our stressors tend to be magnified. Since change is required for a healthy body and mind, we must be aware of how the brain dysregulates and reacts against itself. Be equally diligent in caring for your body as you restore your mind and heart.

September 16

What you see is not often what you get. The unhealed heart comes with a distorted vision from unmet, unfulfilled needs. Unhealed, we search for, want, and expect what we believe is missing. This unquenched life is littered with mirages. Everything looks like a river when we are thirsty for love, understanding, or acceptance. When we get close enough, we see that what we thought would save us is not water at all. Stop walking toward the mirage and learn to sit still and study the art of healing.

September 17

Three frequently used words in the healing process are 'fight,' 'resist,' and 'struggle.' We associate those words with the effort we put forth. However, fighting, resisting, and struggling can quickly become obstacles if we rely on negativity to move us forward. Healing requires us to yield, lean in, and sit with what comes up to become less reactionary and more responsive. Visualize what you want to manifest and make decisions that align with your vision.

Trust the process, be patient, maintain resilience, and affirm your life.

September 18

When life seems to have made us targets for perpetual pain, defensiveness becomes a part of us. Instead of acting upon our wholeness, we react to the world. When our heart is broken, we pick up the shattered pieces and stab the nearest person with the jagged edges. We often do not notice the wounds we create in the world because we have learned to fight with our eyes closed. But the time of healing is upon us. We can open our eyes, minds, and hearts. Allow yourself to be still and feel the peace you have within.

September 19

We can become attached to the struggle and forget what feeling good is like. We can let the good moments go by without acknowledging them, just waiting for the bad to show back up. We notice every single moment of heightened discomfort and remain prepared to respond. We stand ready to retreat or fight. But what do we do when the good moments come? Do we catch up on the "I love you" that we've withheld out of fear? Do we make that phone call to a friend we haven't heard from to check up on them? Do we take healthy risks to move forward? Take time to notice the good so that you can build on it. Pay attention to how you created that experience and use your power to build your healthy reality.

September 20

When we position ourselves to wait, we can leave the door open for unhappiness to enter. We wait for the right person to come along, wait until the money is right, wait for the right time, wait for people to change. Waiting makes you miserable. So, stop waiting and start participating. Go within to figure out what you can control, change, or create in your life. Take action now to decrease your vulnerability to misery. You are an empowered person. Do not accept smallness by waiting on things that you believe are bigger than you. You are the one you have been waiting for.

September 21

Every dysfunction was once a function for survival, or at least your brain thought so. Study the function of your patterns to know why change is so difficult. The belief that you are a bad person has likely been used for survival. The belief that you deserve what you get may have helped you stay alive. There are a hundred scenarios in which dysfunction once served you. So, instead of trying to let go of the negative thought, lean into understanding it.

September 22

Forgiveness is a beautiful experience when it arises after you have done the healing work. Forgiveness does not cause the pain to stop; stopping the pain causes forgiveness. Trying to stop the pain by forgiving is like putting a box of cake mix in the oven and expecting to get a cake. Not only does that not work, but you could burn your house down. Before the oven can do its part, you must first pour out the cake mix, add some ingredients, and stir it up. Forgiveness is similar. You do the work of identifying the dysfunction, practicing love, taking risks, and releasing what does not serve you. Wait until you get to a place where you have all of the ingredients, and healing will occur naturally. Only then will forgiveness serve you well.

September 23

Know your weakness, but live from your strength. Life is not for the perfect, but the daring, the brave, the courageous, the risk-takers, the pioneers, the survivors. Living is participatory. You get to fail and try again, fall and get back up, slip and keep climbing. This is, ironically, how we heal.

September 24

Desire, will, and intention are all required on the healing path. The desire to heal is embedded in all human psyches. No one wants to feel miserable and imprisoned by their mind. Will happens at a deeper level than desire. Will drives behavior and pushes beyond obstacles and excuses to fulfill wishes. Sometimes, our will is not strong enough to manifest our desires. Intention strengthens our will through deep focus. Intention occupies the mind, not through obsession but constant conscious awareness. Intention brings will and desire into alignment. No magic is involved, only work. Assess the alignment of your desire, will, and intention. Where there is a lack of alignment, there is more work to do.

September 25

If you have ever flown, you know the first rule of safety in an emergency. Place your oxygen mask on before you attempt to help others. This is a life-saving tip for those traveling the healing path as well. As much as you may want to save the people who have been traveling through life with you, caring for them may destroy you. Surviving requires you to ignore the instinct to be a martyr and reach for your oxygen mask instead. Don't die trying to save others. Breathe in truth. Breathe in courage. Breathe.

September 26

Building psychological defenses is a little easier when we build physical defenses. Many of us were never permitted to hit or use our voices to scream. We were never granted the right to protect ourselves. Now, however, it isn't too late to build up physical resistance. You can take a self-defense class or work on building muscle right in your own home by doing basic exercises. Focus on being physically stronger in your body and allow your mind to follow.

September 27

Many philosophers, spiritual guides, everyday seekers, and healers are beginning to understand the past, present, and future as intertwined. When something from 20 years ago bothers you, the trigger is in the present. Your past is not troubling you; your present mind is troubled. Some people are troubled by thoughts of the future, but they are troubled in their present minds. Your present mind sends threat signals to you. Repairing those signals does not happen by trying to convince the mind of a linear existence, telling it what belongs in the past. Repairing the signals involves allowing experiences to be addressed in the present. If putting your past behind you isn't working, no worries. That is not a requirement for healing.

September 28

When we hold the belief that we are stronger because of our trauma, we glorify the trauma. When we give pain a purpose, we glorify the trauma. When we create our only positive identity from surviving, we glorify the trauma. Research shows trauma does not make people stronger. Pain compromises the immune system and rewires the brain to mal-adapt. This mentality of glorifying trauma is a "survival of the fittest" attitude. It speaks only of our personal survival and leaves no room to address the social ills that caused the trauma. With this mentality, we ignore the addiction, poor mental health, and poor physical health of survivors, believing pain makes us stronger. If we stop glorifying the trauma, perhaps we can focus more on confronting the systems that create violators.

September 29

We operate within internal and external environments. Often, we focus on a single influence despite there being more than one influence at work. To optimize our lives, we have to evaluate the systems that direct our lives. Depression may be related to a lack of sleep. Your eating habits may be influencing your motivation which influences your chance of success. The friends you choose influence your life-style, which influences your mood, which influences your motivation. Paying attention to our holistic selves is more critical than trying to change any single experience.

September 30

When you look around you, the feelings should be inspiration, collaboration, excitement, and acceptance, maybe even creative and insightful. The feelings certainly should not be fear, isolation, small, unlovable, or dominated. If you are in an environment that consistently brings you negativity, rise up and make changes. Find your words, develop and use your influence, build on your resilience, and manifest change.

October

The Write to Heal

Writing is a well-accepted practice for emotional relief used by mental health professionals. They use a variety of writing techniques to address issues with clients. However, not all writing has the same benefit. Having engaged in just about every form of cathartic writing, I'm quite partial to poetry.

My life looked perfect on the outside, but I felt far from perfect on the inside. I felt irritable and cried for unknown reasons. I had been journaling for three years about my life. Then, one evening before bed, I flipped through my writing pages and realized that every page sounded the same. I was about to write about my day until I realized I had been writing about sadness all along.

I had a Ph.D. in psychology, so I expected to see growth when I looked back on my writing. But, the feelings that prompted me to pick up the journal that night were the same feelings I'd been writing about for three years. I didn't see the point in writing down disappointment and sadness to remind myself about it later. Contrary to popular advice, I have never journaled about my feelings since. However, I did continue to write about my feelings in stanzas and prose. I began to write poetry instead.

I had written poetry on occasion to show appreciation to people.

But, I had never written poetry to process my feelings about being in the world. So, when I opened up my journal on March 15, 2005, I embarked on a different path of healing as I wrote,

> "Invitation."
> As I think, so I may be
> So I'll keep my thoughts hidden,
> So that no one can see—me
> afraid, alone, abandoned.
> The world around me has not been kind,
> Please, someone help me change my mind.
> There's a princess inside me that's tucked so far away.
> I'm hoping tomorrow she will come out to play.
> She's watching and waiting for an invitation
> from peace, love and rejuvenation.

My first poem was basic and unsophisticated. My objective was to write feelings about myself instead of others. When I journaled, I was never self-reflective. I reported my feelings about my husband's inadequate response to me, my disappointment with the ills of the world, or the traits of my body that I didn't like.

Poetry led me on a journey of self-discovery. I stopped reacting to the world when I began exploring myself. The more I wrote, the more I knew about myself and the more responsibility I took for changing my life. Of course, a person's poetry could be just as melancholy as journal writing. If you have ever gone to a poetry open mic, you have witnessed the intense and dark themes of prose. However, there are two distinct advantages that poetry offers.

Being an artist gives a writer much more freedom and creativity than reporting. Writing about feelings requires the brain to return to memories. Creating **poetry** about a feeling can take the writer anywhere. The same is true if the writer starts with the memory. Writing about a memory requires the brain to associate a feeling with the memory. A poem about a memory can take the writer anywhere. They can move into the future or farther back in time before the triggering event. A poem can move the writer entirely away from the event. One poem can offer all three of those spaces.

When I started writing poetry, I became an artist. I could move beyond my depressive identities as a survivor of recent grief and childhood sexual abuse. I felt a responsibility to manage my art rather than report a memory or a feeling. I promised a friend who admired my poetry that once I wrote 50 poems, I would perform at an open mic. My poetry, although she found it inspirational, felt private. Nevertheless, I kept my promise. I have been performing poetry for almost 15 years.

People often ask performance poets why they write such sad poems, or worse, offer pity for our experience. Any poet will give the same response. By the time we perform a poem, the healing has begun, no matter how much emotion we display in the delivery. Sharing poetry deepens the cathartic release. Poets validate themselves by performing, no matter how the audience responds. We leave grief, shame, and self-doubt on the stage. We flaunt the power that we find through picking up the pen. No one shares their journal. The feelings stay caught up between pages for the writer to return to time and time again. As an artist, the next poem is always waiting to carry you beyond the words. We can choose to return to a poem, update it, or share it. So many options exist.

No matter the benefits of poetry, not everyone will relate to it. But, no matter what form of writing is used, therapeutic growth requires the survivor to make connections. Self-exploration is required. The writer has to bypass what is happening in front of them and try to understand what is happening within them. If you write out the details of a painful experience from beginning to end and hold the story close to your heart, then your past is always speaking for you. At first, you may feel a sense of relief. However, depression is likely to return if you have no direction for therapeutic growth. You may only see yourself as a victim.

Therapeutic writing, on the other hand, is purposeful journaling. People often start with a prompt. The prompt can direct people to reconsider the meaning of a past event or visualize a future event as it connects to the present. The purpose may be for the writer to be guided into a sense of personal responsibility or empowerment. There are a few purposeful journaling activities throughout this book.

The absence of memory can be an obstacle to journaling about the past. You can't write what you don't remember. Adult survivors of childhood abuse often experience post-traumatic stress patterns without a precise memory of the harmful events. So, therapeutic journaling should not rely solely on exploring the past. The writing should focus on how the past influences the present rather than writing about the details of the past.

Sharing a **blog** with the world allows for input, which could be good or bad. People can be cruel or kind. So, you have to think carefully about how personal you want to get. You don't have to write about your personal experience. You can write about the healing of trauma and grief in general and still receive some benefits. However, you have a professional obligation to deliver accurate information when speaking outside of personal experience.

The advantage of blogging is the potential support and affirmation that can accrue over time. You build an audience that becomes your fans for life. You can receive affirmation that can neutralize past trauma. Blogs can also turn into **memoirs** over time. I blogged about the healing process for survivors for over five years before I wrote my autobiography. I spent a lot of time and effort becoming an expert while teaching myself how to heal. I wrote daily and rarely shared my personal experience. Reading feedback from subscribers affirmed that I was exploring the relevant issues.

When you blog over a consistent period of time, writing a book may be a natural progression. As you blog, you receive feedback on the receptivity of your writing. You also can feel a regular sense of completion rather than having a year-long project not knowing how it will turn out. The overwhelming majority of books written are read by less than 100 people. So, make sure you are writing your memoir for healing purposes, not followers.

Have a message, not just a story to tell. In my memoir, I told how and why I hid thoughts of suicide. I disclosed accumulating health issues that evolved from my attempt to show success while hiding trauma. I drew on a picture of pain in the absence of the memory of childhood trauma. The message was that "silence is not a quiet space." Your writings along the way, whether blogging, poetry, or therapeutic journaling, have likely formed a theme. Create your message to the world and share it in a book. Healing can occur through many modalities, and a hundred reasons exist for writing. The paths of healing and writing never have to cross. The beauty is when they do.

Activity Ten: I Am Poem

Write an "I Am" poem. The poem must start with the words "I am," but each line may or may not begin with "I Am." Find your flavor.

Include the three stanzas below. Include at least three statements about yourself for each stanza. There is no limit to how long a stanza can be. Have fun and let your creativity flow. Share your poem with someone when you are done.

Stanza 1: What part of your background has influenced the best of who you are.

Stanza 2: What principles you live by.

Stanza 3: Your hopes and dreams for the future.

If you wish to share your poem with me, email it to :
communications@rosennabakari.com

October Daily Gems

October 1

Be proactive and try out new environments. Invite someone new to lunch at work. Visit a different church. Go to the gym at a different time to meet new people. See a movie alone. Take a trip with just one family member who supports you. Make a list of activities, types of people, and outcomes you want to manifest in your life. Then make a plan, a manifesto. You are the change you wish to see in your life.

October 2

Healing is an adopted lifestyle, not an accomplishment. Though they become less and less frequent as we heal, setbacks, triggers, and blind spots are all along the path. Healing isn't measured by days but by the level of peace we are able to secure in our lives and the ability to be present with whatever comes up. We aim to live with authenticity and transparency as we learn to healthfully manage our internal and external responses to the world. Most importantly, we all travel this journey at our own pace and chart our course. The thing we have in common is the journey will last a lifetime.

October 3

We permit ourselves to heal when we permit ourselves to put our needs first; allow people to be disappointed with our decisions and give ourselves room to take risks. We can create joy in our lives, and if we do not know how, we can permit ourselves to learn. People who have never experienced trauma tend to be happy unless something makes them unhappy. People who have experienced trauma from an early age tend to be unhappy unless something makes them happy. We can be our own "something." Just because joy does not show up on its own does not mean we cannot have it. Happiness is something that we can train ourselves to choose each day.

October 4

We design our truth from the authentic remains of our innocence. Restoration of our lives does not come from a book or a therapist, a congregation, or any other relationship. Those are just tools. Healing comes from the heart. In healing, we allow our truth and our narrative to evolve. We cannot always go back and find the truth. Memories get lost, witnesses protect others instead of you, and the pain brings doubt. We have to ask hard questions of people who do not want us to know the answer, consult our inner child whom we had long rejected, and search for words that will not strangle our consciousness. We determine the outlet for our truth by allowing good listeners in.

October 5

Love is simplistically complex, a state of being. Love is not something that you give to or take away from others. Love is a reflection. Like a mirror, you position lovers to reflect your sense of being. Love can have no more demands than you can demand a flower to grow or demand the sun to come out. Love is an act of nature. The feelings that people interpret as love, based on personal experience and cultural values, are fleeting imitations of love. These feelings are based on need, not nature, so they often result in pain. If we truly want to love others or ourselves, we must learn and practice the nature of love.

October 6

There are parts of your growth that may be inconsistent with the religious teachings of your upbringing. Some of the choices you make to move forward may be culturally frowned upon. Decisions in your process may defy family expectations. Finding your own way is OK. Trust the process. Committing to tradition can result in setbacks when you try to walk someone else's path instead of your own.

October 7

One way to effortlessly strengthen our mind is by reading books, not just blurbs. Reading ideas about living well helps us on several levels. Reading stimulates brain cells and can create new learning pathways. Books have an ending, so each book you finish gives you a sense of accomplishment that can boost your confidence. Books help us to increase understanding and change our thinking. Reading books allows us to go at our own pace as we get in touch with our needs. Do not let this be the last book you read for a while. Read more than one book at a time. Stop reading any book that you do not like. There are too many books to choose from to waste time on ones you do not like. Read to learn and learn what to read to move forward in your journey.

October 8

Unhealed, we use the world to determine how OK we are with ourselves instead of using ourselves to determine how OK we are with the world. We obsess over who we can and cannot trust, who does and does not accept us, and who will or will not stay in our lives. The challenge is to love ourselves enough to not need anyone to fill in the gaps of not loving ourselves. To trust ourselves enough not to need anyone to fill in the gap of not trusting ourselves. To be so present with ourselves that we do not need anyone to fill in for us in our lives. That way, when people and opportunities show up to reflect our love and presence, we do not need to cling or fear. When we live inside-out, we just know that we are always OK. We are not always free from pain, but we're always OK because nothing is missing. There is no waiting because we are whole.

October 9

Thrivers ultimately get to a point where we start asking questions of ourselves. We ponder about the sacrifices we are willing to make. We analyze how our beliefs do or do not serve us. We take checks and balances on whom we have given power in our lives. We wonder what we need to do to let our inner child know that we finally hear their pain. We do this contemplation without judgment and from a place of personal power, with or without anger, forgiveness, or fear. Contemplation does not require or result in perfection; it only produces growth.

October 10

The bigger you make people in your world, the smaller you become. To the degree that we hold onto the belief that someone is more important than ourselves, we make ourselves small. We numb ourselves out with addiction, denial, and distraction to ease the pain of fitting into such a small box. That box guarantees that you will never be alone, but the company you keep will always make you wish that you were. That box may guarantee that you will always have someone to talk to but requires your complete silence. That box comes beautifully wrapped on the outside but is full of lies and deception on the inside, which leaves you no room to breathe. So, you suffocate in your tiny box that you call love where there is no room for growth. Getting out requires you to acknowledge your choice to leave, spread your wings, and fly.

October 11

Our mind is preprogrammed for speed over quality of thinking and feeling. Defensive thinking breaks down experiences into their simplest terms, usually based on the first or strongest emotion that is provoked. Typically, the emotion that is provoked is based on past experience. If disappointment is familiar to you, many experiences will be interpreted through the lens of disappointment. It takes reprogramming of our mind to value the quality of thought and feeling over speed. Build up your repertoire of emotions so you have more to choose from. Write a list of emotions that you want to experiment with. With time and practice, you will shift from reactive to responsive.

October 12

When we become attached to a person, we assume the person is attached to us. Instead of seeing our (dysfunctional) attachment, we believe the person has made a life-long commitment to an intense emotional relationship with us. We ignore signs that tell a different story. We continue to move into the relationship, believing that our feelings are the other person's feelings or that our needs are their needs. The trouble is that when we project our feelings onto people, we do not leave room for them to be authentic. We perceive them based only on our needs. Under this circumstance, conflict can quickly arise. We must first be able to offer deep listening and the creation of safe space before expecting it from others.

October 13

We tend to believe that when the time comes, we will do what needs to be done. We tell ourselves, "When I am stronger, more independent, and better supported, I will do what I need to do." Meanwhile, we live with hiding our truth and compromising our values. Still, we do not get what we want and cannot feel what we need. The time has come. The time is now. You can take control of your life with the next decision you make if you commit to making decisions that move you forward. The decision you must make to move forward is the one you've been trying to avoid making.

October 14

Love has lit the path for many to choose the healing journey. We often try to heal for our spouse or for our children. Out of love, we want to be a good partner, parent, or friend. As admirable as that sounds, all of those love relationships are at risk until you begin to heal for yourself. When we love ourselves enough to heal from the inside out, all of our relationships improve. People who cannot tolerate our light will hide from us and people who live in their own light will shine it toward us. Either way, relationships become much less stressful.

October 15

The ability to see beyond yourself aids in the healing process. When the mind stays focused on your tiny world that consists only of your personal experience, you miss the energy and resources found only through understanding the big picture. The little picture has little energy. The big picture has big energy. The world is increasingly global, so we get to experience life with other people. We should not ignore other's pain any more than we like our pain to be ignored. We develop compassion and understanding when we open our hearts to understanding the experience of betrayal, oppression, and disempowerment of all people.

October 16

The inner child can be easily accessed through your pain. Pain exposes our vulnerability and leads us to our inner child. Resistance to vulnerability is resistance to the inner child. You cannot comfort your inner child while you live in denial. You cannot communicate with your inner child and blame the world for your sadness. You cannot heal the inner child and run from their pain. When you seek the inner child, you are making a statement that you are ready to face the pain.

October 17

You cannot love anyone more than you love yourself. The more you love yourself, the more you love others. That includes the number of people you love and how deeply you are capable of loving them. When you do not love yourself, your emotions toward others are full of wanting and expectations. Those expectations and yearnings are so strong that you interpret them as love. But the intensity of emotion is not the same as love. Love allows a person the choice to be in your life or walk out of your life based on their needs. Love leaves you knowing that your self-love is enough to take care of your needs. Love does not target a specific person. Love spreads throughout your community because every time you show up, love is in the room.

October 18

Do not follow the crowd in your pursuit of happiness because most of what you see is an illusion of the mind. We form a culture with an agreement of norms. Norms, in statistical terms, tell us what is likely to work for 68% of the population. Research is based on this concept of norms. That leaves plenty of room for you to operate outside of the norm. More than 30% of people are outside of the norm. There is no path designed specifically for you. You must create your own path.

October 19

Healing is a natural part of human behavior. We cannot return to our original state, but we can return to a natural state of being in the world. We do not crawl through life with hands stretched out, crying for someone to pick us up and carry us, we learn to walk. We learn to speak, communicating our needs and our strengths to the world. Like a flower, rooted where it can bloom in the sunshine, we plant ourselves firmly in communities that strengthen who we are.

October 20

Do not be the scapegoat in your relationships. You may have issues that challenge relationships, but you may also have attracted people who have problems. Since you are on the healing path, chances are you are dealing with your issues more openly than the other people in your life. Your awareness may make you more sensitive to people's behavior, but that is not bad. You should not take the blame for everything wrong in relationships. Holding people accountable for the direction of the relationship is still in our best interest. No one is doing you a favor by being in a relationship with you. You are lovable, and you are enough. Find your voice in everything you do and in every relationship you have.

October 21

When we operate in victim mode with the belief that we are unlovable, we are more likely to attract people who treat us that way. But once we begin to love ourselves unconditionally, we may still feel like we are attracting people who refuse to love us the way we deserve to be loved. We take a bit longer to grow into an understanding that, even when people love us, they respond to us based on their own needs, not ours. Their needs are based on their pain, past, and dysfunctional misperceptions about the world, not just on our relationship with them. We have to maintain enough consciousness to choose who is right for us.

October 22

Despite having reasons for living as you do, you may not be living your best life. The voice that keeps reminding you of your discontent is getting harder to ignore. You feel the desire to live a life of authenticity. You hear the call to find your voice, to stop living in silence at the mercy of others. You see the opportunity to take your power back and return from the walking dead. Everything we do (and do not do) to heal matters. So, stay awake, conscious, and active on the journey. Know where your emotional energy is going. You are more powerful than you realize.

October 23

Triggers are triggers; they are not the problem. Triggers are simply messengers and when our sole focus is on them, we miss the opportunity to move forward. We may reset and steady ourselves, only to find we are standing in the same place. But if we lean into the trigger and show no resistance, we move ahead. If leaning in seems too risky to do on your own, seek professional help. Most triggers, however, are not traumatic. They leave us shaken, confused, anxious, bitter or enraged, but not in despair. Instead of focusing so much on what the trigger was and how we reacted (which is one important aspect, but only one), we can go deeper to explore what needs to be healed. Learn to use triggers as a pointer, making them significant instead of just scary.

October 24

When we carry guilt and shame through secrets, we can never really trust others to love us. Even more difficult is trusting ourselves to love ourselves, regardless of who chooses to love us. Guilt keeps us from loving and accepting ourselves, and we cannot invite people into an empty space of love. In a state of guilt, we do not believe people's attempts to love us because we know that they only love what we show. We believe that they would not love our hidden parts. Our lack of trust can cause defensive conversations, jealous thinking, possessive expectations, and emotional distance from a partner. When you let go of the secrets that cause you guilt or shame, you will feel a shift within that will create changes in relationships. The shift will not make relationships perfect, but it will make them more authentic, whether with family members, lovers, or close friends.

October 25

There is nothing we're currently good at that we started out being good at. We move from having an interest in something to giving it a try. We go from trying it to getting better, and then to getting good, and eventually to 'feeling like a natural.' When we 'feel like a natural,' our skill has grown to be better than most. While getting better than most takes minimal effort, we still had to move through a process to get there. Chances are you have experienced this. You read something interesting and paid attention to it every chance you got. You talked about it a lot and shared the experience with other people. You took risks to get better at it, maybe invested money and time to access professional help or coaching. You probably altered your lifestyle to accommodate it. Well, you are facing a similar journey to healing.

October 26

Our fear of expressing, demanding, or appreciating bodily autonomy affects how we treat our bodies. If you do not see your body as fully belonging to you, caring for the body becomes difficult. We are less likely to look at our bodies when we do not express autonomy. We simply command the body to transport our busy minds. We fear getting too attached to our body lest someone comes along and destroys it. Perhaps you live in fear of your beauty, sensuality, or physical power. If you hope to reclaim your mind, you have to reclaim your bodily autonomy.

October 27

Acknowledging pain does not make you weak; it makes you human. Hiding pain makes you weak because too many of your brain cells are being used to keep secrets and play pretend. Not forgiving someone will not destroy your soul. Forgiving another person while you hate yourself will destroy your soul. Being angry will not eat your insides. Denying yourself the right to be angry will eat your insides. Processing your past will not keep you stuck. Ignoring your past will keep you stuck in unhealthy patterns. Let go of these lies, acknowledge your pain, love yourself, allow your anger, and process your past.

October 28

There is a difference between *feeling* accepted and *being* accepted. Feeling accepted is based on the roles that you play for others. Being accepted is based on who you are. Being accepted does not require you to be any other way than what you are while inviting you to be your best. But you cannot spin your wheels trying to find people who accept you for who you are. You have to be who you are and allow people to find you in that space of authenticity and transparency. Practice being liked by you. Build a relationship with yourself so that you still feel loved if no one else comes into that space. You build a relationship with yourself by focusing on what is happening within you — the good, the bad, and the ugly — rather than focusing on what is happening around you.

October 29

Healing is not something that feels better every day, even though we make progress every day. The decisions we make to heal are painful at times. The changes we make are awkward at first. People move in and out of our lives as we transition from victim to survivor and we have to adjust. Every aspect of our lives is touched by our attempts to heal. We should not judge our progress only on days that we struggle or in only one area of our lives. We should not judge our progress based on where we want to be. Instead, when we accept healing as a lifestyle and a lifelong journey, we permit ourselves to be OK every day.

October 30

As long as we live in truth, we do not need to try to shove anything down someone's throat. We have enough healing of our own to do without trying to take responsibility for someone else's ignorance. The more we live in our truth, the less space we leave for lies, no matter how comfortable we perceive them to be. We accepted lies about ourselves and the world because we didn't know better. But, once you know, you know. We invite others into a space of healing with truth, staying unattached to the invitation. Meanwhile, we won't choose to live a life of smallness.

October 31

No matter what type of therapy you seek, you must remember that you are your own healer. Be suspicious of people who claim to heal you, whether they use energy work, cognitive restructuring, or talk therapy. The helper is a helper. The healing must come from within with the guidance of the helper. However, if you look to be saved, you are vulnerable to becoming attached to external resources, even therapists. Great therapists work themselves out of a job rather than convincing clients to cling to them as the source of healing. Make sure you recognize the therapist as the tool for healing, not the healing source. You are the source of your own healing.

November

How to Re-parent Your Inner Child

Your inner child has been trying to get your attention for a long time. You've been too busy with life to notice. You have a grown-up pace to keep up with work, relationships and maintaining good impressions. You have been the go-getter. Keeping busy is how you've survived. However, the go-getter still lives with a sense of insignificance and unworthiness.

So many adults have suffered from childhood trauma. Being a child did not feel safe, and they had to grow up quickly. As adults, they remain distant from their inner child. Still, the inner child is always looking out through the peephole of your heart, the window of your survivor's eyes, and the crack in your pain. Just because you can't see in doesn't mean they can't see out. The inner child sees what you are committed to, feels what you use as a distraction, and hears every thought. Time is always ticking.

My wake-up call from my inner child came at age 44. A loving marriage with children, solid community reputation, and successful career were all jeopardized when my childhood trauma resurfaced. I found myself balled up in a fetal position, lying on the bathroom floor, crying over 40-year-old pain. No degree of success made me permanently immune to suffering. I sought a nontraditional therapist who dug deep into my subconscious, not to recover memories but to find my inner child that held them. I thought my inner child's vulnerability was my curse and her beauty a snare for dangerous attention from men. Ultimately, I had to understand the trauma and psychological demand placed upon my internal seven-year-old.

No matter how functional our behavior may be, unaddressed trauma may interfere with psychological comfort or physical health and create "dis-ease." Wounded inner child experiences may manifest in adulthood as depression and anxiety or a compromised immune system such as asthma. The field of research called "adverse childhood experiences" indicates ten common childhood experiences that, when combined, have negative effects on the adult experience. Those experiences include non-contact experiences of the child such as single parenting, mental disturbances, imprisonment, and domestic violence, as well as direct physical, emotional, or sexual abuse. The more adverse experiences an adult endured during childhood, the more likely they are to have heavy mental and physical health burdens.

Adults who were exposed to four or more adverse childhood experiences have considerably more difficulties than people who have less than four. Those with four or more are far more likely to have severe health conditions, higher than average mental health visits each year, and an increase in broken relationships. Many survivors of adverse childhood experiences behave childishly in adulthood. Their thinking is centered around themselves as they are unable to see or understand any perspective but their own. They look to defend themselves, physically and mentally. Childish adults constantly seek affirmation, conformity, or acceptance no matter the cost.

Healthy adulthood does not come easy when your childhood was uneasy. The unfulfilled desire to be chosen, cared for, or rescued, can result in investing in trauma-bonding-relationships, a lack of risk-taking to secure the future, and even unintentionally harmful parenting patterns. Happy, peaceful, independent adulthood hinges on acknowledgment and acceptance of your inner child, along with taking responsibility for re-parenting your inner child. Fortunately, the inner child remains accessible throughout adulthood.

Many psychotherapists focus on healing the inner child to improve adult mental health. Where significant adverse childhood experiences disempower survivors, they often feel unlovable, insignificant, and fear abandonment. Their success is often accomplished from a position of fear. Fear can produce overachievement and independence, as well as high tolerance of emotional pain. However, when they are buried beneath decades of distraction and denial, the inner child is difficult to reach.

I had a great deal of success before age 44, achieved by my resilience. But my success was based on hiding my trauma instead of healing it. Today, healing allows me to live with authenticity and transparency that acknowledges my pain. When I acknowledged the pain of my inner child, I stopped going to family events where my pain was ignored. I stopped shifting my truth to make others comfortable. Three years into my healing I started a nonprofit organization to support other survivors on the healing journey. Ten years into my healing I started another business to empower women. I became a writer and motivational speaker. Healing meant that I was no longer using invisibility as a superpower.

The inner child has a place in our adult lives. Becoming childlike (not childish) is the most adult thing we can do on the healing journey. People who are childlike laugh and take more risks, and are more active and carefree. They are more at ease with uncertainty. Think about a skill or talent you developed in childhood. That talent is connected to your inner child. Maybe it's time to pick it back up. It may help you become conscious of your inner child. Invite your inner child into the realm of creativity and expression. Start by ordering an adult coloring book online. If you want to revive your musical interest and can't afford a piano, purchase a keyboard. If you have children in your house, play with them. Instead of getting them to do more adult chores and activities, introduce them to your inner child. Try to laugh with them each day. Watch cartoons, tell silly jokes, jump on the bed and have a pillow fight. Your inner child will thank you.

In addition to giving your inner child an expression in your life, you must also re-parent your inner child. Re-parenting is not the same as nurturing your inner child. Nurturing your inner child requires affirmation and allowing space for your vulnerability. Re-parenting your inner child involves offering quality care based on childhood needs.

Our inner child's needs don't change. Self-sufficiency, predictability, reliability, and consistency are required for proper development. When children are raised with consistency, reliability, and predictability, they navigate more seamlessly through adulthood. They manage relationships well, take reasonable risks, and look to give from a place of love, not out of fear of abandonment or feeling inadequate.

When we live according to predictable patterns, we show respect for past outcomes. In particular, we avoid repeating mistakes. Life is fairly predictable. If your family members hurt your feelings every time you gather, respect that fact instead of giving it one more try. Make choices based on known information rather than adult denial. When the adult insists on trying to fit in, the inner child suffers.

Gift your inner child the experience of good predictions. Don't try to convince your inner child that something is going to turn out differently if you don't do something differently. You have to make good choices, not familiar ones. Your inner child will learn to trust your re-parenting when you honor predictability.

Reliability is equally important. The more you surround yourself with unreliable people, the more you will recreate the trauma of your inner child. Unreliability creates instability in your growth, and you will continue to take two steps forward and one step back.

People with active trauma are more likely to be unreliable. If they haven't learned self-management, they may negatively react when their needs are unmet. Moreover, if either of you grows, you will outgrow the relationship because trauma bonds need trauma identities. Who you surround yourself with matters, so stop building bonds based on trauma.

If you do have unreliable people in your life, do not rely on them. They may be good for pop-up visits and birthday parties, but that's it. Don't give them any significant role in your life. Obey the law of predictability.

Consistency is more about what you do to show up for yourself.

The changes you make in your life must be consistent. You have to discipline yourself to show up for your inner child who needs to learn to trust you. Many survivors abandon their inner child whenever their life is comfortable. They only turn to the healing journey when their pain is triggered by external circumstances. This pattern reinforces emotional immaturity and prolongs the healing process.

Effort and responsible risk-taking must be consistent. Say no to the company of people who always trigger your inner child. Offer quality care to yourself on a scheduled basis. Engage in healing communities consistently, not just when you need support. You must constantly look for new insights about yourself and your growth.

You must be active in your healing. Otherwise, you will get off track and repeat bad patterns. Most people only think about healing when something hurts. As soon as they find something to make them feel better (like a new relationship, job, or friends), they stop their healing activities. They crawl back to the healing journey only when things inevitably go wrong again.

Allowing yourself to be surprised or indignant about repeated actions will force your child to remain hidden and silent. On the contrary, it is when you consistently choose your inner child that you will release yourself from the desire to be chosen. Choose self-affirming desires, thoughts, and actions. You must show up for your inner child as their responsible parent and loving guide.

Activity Eleven: Record and Meditate

Record the following meditation on your phone.

1. Use a softer than normal voice.

2. You may add smoothing music in the background.

3. Take your time for an error-free recording.

4. Complete a 21-day practice of listening twice a day in a restful state. You may sit comfortably or lie down.

> *"Free your mind from the burden of misguided nurturance. Where your childhood care defied human nature, social expectation, and spiritual consciousness, you are still lovable. You are enough.*
>
> *For, though you came from the wound, not just the womb, of a woman, you were manifested by the universe. Your spirit is ancient, not anxious; wise, not weary. You exist, not because a woman delivered you, but because a goddess ordered you. Before your mother's mother was formed, you existed. The physical portal to which you entered this world does not represent your true value in this space and time.*

The purpose of this space is to support your truth about your past and affirm your certainty about your future. You deserve to heal. You are more than your mother's daughter. You are the descendant of the universe itself.

What you hear in this space today may not resonate completely today. But, it will someday. So, you don't need to try to force your mind to understand everything. For, I am not speaking to your mind. I am addressing your heart, the heart that existed before the mind formed.

As I speak today, I want you to focus on the present, even as you explore the past. Acknowledge the influence of the past on your present. But that acknowledgment must be a commitment to release. Are you ready to release the psycho-social-emotional connection to the womb that was your portal to the present world? When you release your attachment to the concept of "mother, family, or caregiver," you will cultivate the nurturance you deserve.

For, though you came from the wound, not just the womb, of a woman, you were manifested by the universe. Your spirit is ancient, not anxious; wise, not weary. You exist, not because a woman delivered you, but because a goddess ordered you. Before your mother's mother was formed, you existed. The physical portal to which you entered this world does not represent your true value in this space and time."

November Daily Gems

November 1

There is a difference between strength and resistance. Strength uses whatever resources are required for survival. Strength is required when survival is at stake. Attention and precision are required for the execution of strength. Resistance is made up of patterned responses to perceived threats, whether the threat is there or not. When you use resistance, you adapt your life to your patterns. When you use strength, you adapt your patterns to your life. Beneath the vulnerability of the inner child lies great strength that can only be accessed through self-love. You have to move beyond resistance (back to strength) to find her/him.

November 2

Our bodies have a right to feel pleasure. If our psychological pain is attached to shame, we deny ourselves the right to receive pleasure. We may detach from or punish ourselves through the body. We may only allow ourselves to connect to our bodies through destructive patterns instead of harmony with ourselves. But healing the body can help heal the mind. There are all sorts of beautiful sensations we can expose our bodies to. Sharing intimate touch is just one of them. Looking at your body in the mirror with loving affirmation is an important way to connect. Getting the right amount of sleep can bring body harmony as well. Pay attention to the experience of your body and let your body matter. Treat yourself to sensual pleasure, not just sex. Having a body is what makes us human beings. Allow yourself to enjoy the experience.

November 3

There are some hard truths that we must face as we heal. One hard truth is that we do not hurt because people mistreat us; we hurt because we invest so much into people out of fear of being alone. When our investment in them fails, we return to the pain that existed before we engaged in the distraction disguised as a relationship. We repeat the cycle of investments that lead to emotional bankruptcy in relationships. The more relationships fail, the less we tend to value ourselves. On the other hand, the more we value or trust ourselves, the less vulnerable we become to mistreatment.

November 4

You can do a ton of strength training to gain beautiful strong muscles. However, if you want the honor of actually seeing those beautiful muscles, you must lose weight and become lean. Fat hides muscle, making it impossible to notice the work that you have done to be strong. So, it is with our healing path. You have done plenty to build resilience. But you carry too much weight for your work to be noticed. You carry the weight of trying to maintain family relationships that deny your pain. Your stretch marks grow with the weight of conformity. Your muscle definition of resilience is hidden by the unnecessary fat in your life. Go lean and flex your resiliency muscles.

November 5

Turning attention inward is the most challenging aspect of healing. Every time things are going well in our lives, we tend to think that we have healed more than we have. We think that we've done the work and that the work is over, so we stop looking within. But when the slightest difficulty arises it seemingly triggers a setback. But the "setback" is just showing you what healing is left to be done. You never did the work of going within to heal. Instead, you found the perfect distraction from the work, and the distraction was interrupted. Making the work internal is what makes healing enduring in our lifelong journey.

November 6

Healing is not based on forgiveness. You get to decide who you forgive, but you must start with yourself. "No contact" is not a definitive stance. You choose the exact level of family contact that is best for your mental health. You determine how to practice self-care in relationships based on your own needs. Leaving a relationship does not mean you are not willing to grow. Staying does not mean that you have grown. Healing is not black and white. So, consider deeply what the world tells you is best for you. Ask yourself: who benefits from norms and customs? Who holds power or makes progress as a result of you sticking to norms? Norms have never been truly humane. So, feel free to break them along with your silence.

November 7

Taking back your power gives you control over your own life, but not over others. Power is not about changing others but acting on our own behalf. The person you have to confront first is yourself. Stop being your own bully. Stop intentionally making yourself unattractive, saying bad things about yourself to other people, denying yourself the right to emotions, refusing to look in the mirror, apologizing for taking up space or time, etc. When people see your attempt to hide your attractiveness, they may tell you that you are attractive, and then you mistake their perception for love and offer them your power. When someone hears you criticize yourself constantly, they know that compliments are your weakness, and they take your power away with kindness that never lasts. Deny your emotions, and someone will play on them until you give up your power. Taking back your power starts with how you treat yourself.

November 8

Tradition says you should live the virtue of forgiveness in hopes that you will have peace. But the peace never comes, and you continue to live in hell on earth. Forgiveness may help people look "normal" and spare reputations, but their minds and hearts are not spared. If no pain has been acknowledged, no space to heal has been offered, and no reparation has been made, forgiveness can do more harm than good. Forgiveness does not cause healing. Healing causes forgiveness.

November 9

As you grow out of fear and grow into living from a place of love, you begin to try new behaviors. Here are a few behaviors to play with if you are not already doing them. Try looking people in the eye because eye contact fosters trust and invites engagement. Sharing moments of silence instead of filling every second with noise. Shared silence strengthens relationships. Verbalize gratitude with words like please and thank you so people know you appreciate them. As you stop seeking validation from outside of yourself, your external behaviors become more empowering. Step into your light.

November 10

Emotions are our tools to build experiences. If you ask the average person to name as many tools as they can in ten seconds, you will likely get a hammer, drill, screwdriver, and maybe a saw. If you ask them how many tools they know how to use, that list likely shortens to screwdriver and hammer. The average person knows little about building anything because they know so little about the tools required for building. If you go into Home Depot, you will find hundreds of tools, so you must know what you are trying to build or repair before you choose your tools. The same can be said for personal experiences. If your emotional tool knowledge is limited to happy, angry, and sad, your ability to build will be quite limited. Practice the language of emotions to build stronger relationships.

November 11

Do not glorify pain as a necessary ingredient for growth. There is a big difference between natural pain and human-created pain. We need nature to take its course, but the pain humans create defies nature and impedes human growth and development. We can trace every mass destruction back to pain. Yet, we continue to maintain the lie that pain causes growth. Pain is not a blessing. We were not created to endure pain. The world can rid itself of pain only if we stop glorifying it.

November 12

No one has to teach a child how to love themselves. Human brains are wired to love ourselves. "Not Loving Oneself" is what's taught. If you were taught to not love yourself, learning self-love as an adult is like learning a foreign language as we age. The learning curve is steep. We have to immerse ourselves in the language of self-love to become proficient. Spend time in environments that speak the language of love. Read books, watch television, socialize around the experience of love. Avoid environments that encourage your first language of conflict, criticism, doubt, and confusion. That is the language of "other." We want to master the language and life of self, "self-love."

November 13

Personal power grows with experience. The more you succeed, the more confident you become. However, success inherently involves setbacks, mistakes, and failure. Successful people separate the failure of the event from the failure of the person. You can fail one hundred times on your way to success if you allow your failures to redirect you through self-examination instead of stopping you through self-judgment.

November 14

Most of what we need to better our lives is within us. The choices we make, the activities we choose, where we dedicate our time, and what we feed our mind are life's ingredients. They can yield negative or positive results. We must shop wisely for our life-recipe ingredients if we desire peace. Your inner world is like a superstore. Everything you need is in there. The trick is knowing what you need and where to find it. You have to go within to see it, whatever it is.

November 15

There is a difference in accommodating pain versus healing from pain. Make sure you are healing, not just accommodating the pain. Some of us adapt to the pain so well that we start to choose familiar dysfunction over unfamiliar healthy choices. Being out of control in some way feels freer than using our energy to manifest the life we deserve. Giving over control to substances, people, jobs, or our children feels freer than making conscious choices. When we relinquish control, we feel free to blame someone when things do not work out for us. We feel free to hold someone else responsible for our discontent. We are accommodating pain by asking someone to carry our pain in exchange for controlling our lies (I mean life). This deal is self-sabotage. Putting your healing in the hands of anything or anyone is self-sabotage. The only way out is to walk the path on your own two feet.

Real helpers will hold your hand, but be suspicious of anyone who offers to carry you.

November 16

Darkness may hide the path, but the path still exists. All that is required is a little light. The less light you have, the more focus you need to see the path. Just like when you turn off all of the lights to sleep at night, you do not worry that your closet is still there, full of your clothing. You apply your understanding of the physical world to ease your mind. Well, there is an equally important understanding of the "spiritual" world that tells us the healing path is always present, even when we are in darkness.

November 17

The term "somatoform" is coming into the mainstream. The term is used to describe physical symptoms that cannot be explained by medical causes, i.e. symptoms without a cause. Sometimes people are offended by a somatoform diagnosis because they interpret the doctors as saying "It's all in your head." "It's all in your head" suggests that what you are experiencing is not real at all, that you are imagining your pain. However, this is not at all what somatoform means. A somatoform diagnosis fully recognizes that the illness or pain is present. The diagnosis is meant to recognize that emotional trauma can cause a physical response. Instead of the pain being caused by something medical, the cause is psychological. It suggests that in order for our body to heal itself, we have to address what is in our head. Our body does not function independently of our mind. The doctor can treat the symptoms, but only the brain can cure them.

November 18

There is a bigger picture that influences how we heal our smaller lives. Selflessness is an imperative component for healing. When we heal with a purpose, we heal faster because we can synchronize our healing with the world's healing. We do not try to heal the world instead of ourselves. We commit to healing the world as we heal ourselves. Most of the problems of the world are related to oppression. We just have to choose our focus. When we can see others' oppression, we become clearer about how we participate in the world. We create a pathway to go within where we begin to find "answers."

November 19

Since the universe saw fit for you to be here another day, seize the day. Dying was not the option; giving *up* is not an option. So, don't let giving *in* be an option. You do not need any more power than you already have. You do not need permission. You can decide what will get you one step further on the healing path today. Perhaps you need to use your voice to express your self-responsibility. Maybe you need to take a risk to show your fearlessness. Maybe you need to reach out to share your resilience. Seize the day.

November 20

Your personal resources include time, intimacy, money, and possessions. The more access you give a person to these things, the more you should be able to expect in return. In return for any of these resources, you might get some sort of joy or advancement in some area of your life. Adults with good boundaries take informal measurements of these exchanges. They do not allow people to consistently take up their time, enter their intimate space, use their possessions, or access their money just to avoid being alone or out of fear of abandonment. There has to be positive value-added in order to enter their boundary of vulnerability. Healthy adults are vulnerable by decision and choice, not out of fear. When you do not protect your boundaries, then vulnerability is a weakness. When you protect your boundaries, then vulnerability is power. Think consciously about your resources and who you offer access to. When you operate with healthy intentions, you will have healthy boundaries.

November 21

Healing is always personal. But sometimes healing is political as well. Disempowered people tend not to see themselves as game-changers. When you empower yourself through healing (not fear), you see your potential to empower others. When you see your potential, you grow into your personal power. Power creates, fear destroys. Power produces love, fear produces hate. Power helps heal, fear causes wounds. Each of us can look within and determine when we are finding our power or feeding our fear.

November 22

The good news is that everything *does* get better on the healing path. The bad news is that some things have to fall apart before they get better. If your air conditioner stops working, you call a repair person. When they arrive, they do not flip a switch. Most repairs require some level of dismantling first. The dismantling looks worse than the original problem and is indeed worse if you do not complete the project. There is a lot of dismantling in the early stages of healing, which starts when you stop hiding. You have to trust the process and stay engaged in it on a daily basis. The "better" part comes with time when you apply deep intention.

November 23

Boundaries go both ways for healthy adults. When you respect your own boundaries, you are unlikely to push your way through other people's boundaries. Begging for attention, pleading to be noticed, and demanding to be first are ways of disregarding boundaries that people set for you. Love that is not offered freely will always cost too much. Healing moves us into a flow of life and out of conflict, out of seeking, out of waiting to be rescued. Saying no feels healthy, not scary. Drawing the line is a statement of self-love, not an invitation for conflict. Be accepting when people let you know where you stand. Make your next move from a place of self-love instead of a place of regret.

November 24

If we measure our healing by the disappearance of all negative patterns of survival, then we will feel hopeless. If our expectation of healing is a permanent life of comfort, then we set ourselves up for failure. Healing is more about the way we approach life than the actual outcome. Healing is a commitment to live authentically, transparently, and unapologetically, where we only attempt to control ourselves and no one else. Healing is an acceptance of living life on life's terms rather than a life of "should" and "if." Healing is the responsibility to make your life your own, *by design* rather than settle for a life dictated by trauma.

November 25

There are times that you feel joy, happiness, contentment, bliss, delight, or appreciation that go unnoticed. Positive feelings can get ignored by a hyper-vigilant, over-active, defensive mind. If you only have a hammer, all you notice are the nails sticking out. Make a shift to notice everything, not just what feels like a threat. This is not the same as positive thinking or gratitude. This is about awareness. We get closer to our authentic selves with understanding. You are already aware of the threats. Be equally aware of when your mind and body feel at ease. Allow yourself to relax. Give your mind permission to smile, lower your voice, say thank you, notice what part of your body is not in pain, touch someone with care and intentionality, etc.

November 26

Fill yourself with love, acceptance, and significance. Pour your own serving and let your cup runneth over. That way, when people enter your life, you can develop relationships based on your fullness, not your emptiness. You will have love to share instead of looking for love to affirm you. That way, as people come and go, you are still whole, complete, significant. You are not broken. No one needs to fix you. Your heart and mind are beautiful. You just have to learn to redirect them inward. The reason the healing journey does not have a destination is that the travel is inward. Keep going until you find yourself, no matter how beautiful the scenery of others.

November 27

When you *give* yourself to someone, regret often follows. That goes for your body too. When you *share* yourself with someone, growth often follows. When healing, we must pay careful attention to our actions to know when we are giving versus sharing. When you give, the receiver can do what they choose with what is given. When you share, you make decisions about what is being shared. Intimacy is an experience of shared consent. There are a lot of decisions that should be shared in intimacy, such as when to approach, how to approach, and the protection used. Just these three decisions may have to be made several times, depending on the duration of the activity. If there is no conversation of consent before and during intimacy, you are likely giving (or taking) instead of sharing. Of course, the consequence is constantly reliving or acting out the abuse patterns as a child, a significant obstacle to healing.

November 28

Finding happiness in the morning is essential to how you experience your day. When you open your eyes in the morning, think about how you feel. No conflict has occurred. No one has gotten in your way, talked badly toward you, or asked you for anything you didn't want to give. As soon as you open your eyes, notice how you feel. If you open your eyes with a sense of worry, fear, and unease, you will pay attention to the experiences that validate those feelings. So, before you get out of bed, comfort yourself with affirmations. Say one for yourself and for everyone you share the home with. Set the intention to move about your day fully present.

November 29

When we release people from the expectation of responding to us in a specific way, we also free ourselves from conditional silence. We speak when our hearts and minds are ready to release the secret and let words wash away the shame. We disclose when we are prepared to hold people accountable for their actions and honor our survival. We cannot prepare the listener, we can only prepare our voice. We lead with our vulnerability and acknowledge a fear of rejection, knowing that leaning into the unknown is where we will find our strength. When our voice is no longer connected to the need for the perfect listener, we begin to roar.

November 30

Thoughts are how we survive, but they are not who we are. We do not have to control our thoughts. Research shows that trying to control negative thoughts makes them stand out even more. There are hundreds of thoughts in our heads at any given time. Instead of accepting whatever thought comes to consciousness, we can *choose* our thoughts. Living well is a recipe. You choose the thoughts that go with your life recipe. Determine what is healthy for your life and choose the thoughts you need for that recipe. If you are baking a cake and open up your cabinet and the first thing you see is garlic, you know you have to look past the garlic to get the baking soda. You do not fear the garlic and throw it away. The same goes for our thoughts. You have to choose the thought that goes with what you are trying to make of your life.

December

How to Capture The Wellness of Sexual Energy

I would be remiss if I left the topic of sexual satisfaction out of a book on wellness and relationships. Sexual pleasure can significantly increase relationship satisfaction and wellness. Yet, a 2015 online survey of more than 1000 women using the "Healthy Women / Lippe Taylor Women's Health Behavior Index" confirmed ongoing concerns about the female sexual experience.

According to survey results, 60% of women want more sex, although only 27% of women orgasm with every intercourse encounter. The rate increases to 34% with oral sex. Women's overall orgasm rate is 69% when partnering with men, compared to 95% for men in heterosexual encounters. The rate for women is significantly higher in same-sex encounters. Sadly, women's lack of sexual satisfaction with men is a cultural norm embedded within a system that emphasizes a particular power structure. That structure entitles only men to orgasm despite the fact that the female body is particularly designed for orgasm, as the clitoris has no other function.

Women have fought robustly to remove power structures that restrict economic success. Yet, research reveals that women compromise their body autonomy to fulfill their partners' sexual desires, including agreeing to have 'threesomes,' watching pornography, and performing as bisexual at parties. Women use social scripts to rationalize these often coercive sexual experiences along with sex without orgasm.

There are significant physical and emotional benefits to orgasm. Oxytocin and endorphins are released during orgasm, which can contribute to more confidence and less depression. No wonder married men live longer and are more successful than unmarried men. Meanwhile, many women may be missing out on the benefits of orgasm and the empowerment it can bring. Some women intend to trade orgasm for alternative benefits such as time, loving attention, and gifts from their partners that make them feel valued. Those expectations often go unmet. For women and men who are ready to shift the narrative of the single-orgasm sexual experience, the language they use around body autonomy is important during intimacy.

The old assumptions that placed males at the center of sex should be updated with an ideology of partnering, which relies on communication. The language of sex can feel as awkward as learning to speak any foreign language. However, the shift in power dynamics is at stake. The language of sexual communication only works with a mental shift in the relationship around power and passion. The shift has to start with an acceptance that women are equally entitled to an orgasm. Men have an equal responsibility to engage in sex with the intent to deliver pleasure, not just receive it. Even when you make this mental shift, it doesn't come with words. Effective communication or directives do not automatically accommodate the shift. The pleasure scripts have to be rewritten. The following five script updates can increase sexual satisfaction for partners ready to engage one another beyond traditionally oppressive roles.

"We have to use protection." Partners have a right to protect themselves from unwanted consequences, particularly pregnancy and disease. Research says that women with economical and educational disadvantages and underage women are more likely to experience sex without protection and more likely to suffer negative consequences. The Center of Disease Control 2017 report on sexually transmitted diseases shows a sharp increase in STDs in the overall population since 2013.

Sex should not be an expression of power that puts individuals at risk. Sex is a partnering experience, and partners communicate. Communicating about risks is a good place to start. Moreover, taking an unwanted risk out of the situation may allow for a more relaxed experience, which increases the likelihood of female orgasm.

"I need more touching" is important to convey to a partner and important for a partner to respect. If a partner does not respect this request, then consent is not happening - compliance maybe, but not consent. There is a difference between consent and compliance. Compliance is about avoiding consequences, part of the traditional paradigm that compromises female body autonomy, or lack thereof. When partners comply to avoid a negative response, they are disempowered. The sexual experience has to be equally empowering for all partners. Women should not be expected to be donors of pleasure. Consent is about engaging in pleasure. Both partners should be participants in sexual pleasure and enthusiastically agree on the level of protection, positions, location, and variety of intimacy.

Although foreplay lasts an average of 15 minutes, there is no limit to how much touching a woman should have before she is ready for genital contact or penetration. Women generally desire longer foreplay than men but are reluctant to ask for it. However, men who want to partner, not dominate, are willing to acquiesce to a woman's desire. If a partner ignores a request for more touching, then sexual pleasure is likely not the only problem in the relationship. You may have to fix the power dynamics in other areas of your relationship to improve your sexual experience.

"Help me orgasm first." Since intercourse ends with the male orgasm, the female orgasm should occur before penetration. "Female first" may be the biggest, most essential shift in the sexual experience. The requirement for females to orgasm before penetration immediately levels the sexual experience.

If couples withheld penetration until after the woman orgasmed through other stimulation, the ratio of male-to-female orgasm encounters would be equal. What a simple solution! Women have been conditioned to be used as objects of sexual pleasure rather than subjects of sexual pleasure. So, a serious mental shift in both men and women must take place for these words to be used.

Traditional sex scripts place the penis at the center of the sexual experience. So, some men are less inclined to use their hands and mouths to produce female orgasm, much less to prioritize female orgasm. Consequently, despite women being physiologically capable of experiencing multiple orgasms, many of them experience none. Research shows that men invest in their partner's orgasm according to the level of commitment to the relationship. In hook-up sex, women orgasm only 40% of the time, whereas married women orgasm in more than 75% of encounters with male spouses. Women earn the right to sexual pleasure whereas men are entitled to it.

You must control the centrality of the sexual experience with clear communication. Female orgasm before penetration is a reasonable request. The clitoris is not a glitch. It has twice the nerve endings than the head of the penis and contributes significantly to the outcome of the sexual experience. In addition to the clitoris, nipples and the G-spot can also be stimulated to produce orgasm without the penis. You can show and tell your partner how to make sure you both experience orgasm.

"Don't come yet" may be intimidating words associated with sex for men, second only to "I love you." However, the request also means the woman is enjoying the experience. The degree to which males can delay their orgasm varies, but practice makes perfect. Men who have never been asked to delay an orgasm may not be capable of it at first. Men who are fully invested and practiced in gratifying their partner may be quite good at it. Co-creating brings a balance of power to the sexual experience.

Requesting a man to both delay orgasm and ensure female orgasm before penetration may sound like double-dipping. It is double-dipping, and there is nothing wrong with it. Any man who complains about his partner having multiple orgasms should check in with his patriarchal assumptions and social expectations. The female orgasm is a way to engage her in the sexual experience as a subject rather than an object. It is not a cue for the male to 'take his turn.'

Many women accept synchronized orgasm with their partner as the ultimate sexual experience instead of requesting their partner to delay his orgasm for her sexual pleasure to continue. Females feel privileged instead of entitled to orgasm when they get to ride the coat tail of the male ejaculation. But, at the deepest level of partnering, both partners negotiate when sex begins and when it ends.

"I want to switch positions" is important to the practice of body autonomy and should be a welcomed request. A woman's body changes throughout the monthly cycle. So, even if she achieved an orgasm in a particular position a week ago, the same position may not feel as stimulating. Finding the right degree of stimulation based on the positioning may be trial and error and result in multiple interruptions during intimacy. However, it may increase female orgasm quality and quantity.

Switching positions may also bring greater comfort to females based on body image. Bodies appear differently in prone positions than kneeling over a partner. Women who are concerned with body image may prefer particular positions. Women who are embarrassed to advocate for more desirable positioning during intimacy may be complying with sex instead of consenting. Men who do not honor a request to switch positions may be forcing compliance instead of adhering to the rules of consent.

The sexual experience is a partnership. Sex is not something that one person gives or takes from another. It should not require females to be orgasm martyrs. Female orgasms should not be considered any more optional than male orgasms. Communication must penetrate the sexual experience to break free of the traditional bedroom scripts that place females as objects with compromised body autonomy. The language of sexual communication may be as awkward as creating new sounds with your tongue to speak a foreign language. Yet, practice is the only way we learn. The more we immerse ourselves in the language of intimacy, the more comfortable it becomes.

Activity Twelve: Mirror, Mirror

Have notepaper and pen handy before you start. Stare at yourself in the mirror for 30 seconds without looking away. Set the timer on your cell phone so you know when the time is up. Try to keep eye contact with yourself the entire time. When the time is up, reset your timer for another 30 seconds.

Immediately, and for the next 30 seconds, write down what you feel without stopping. You will get your best results of introspection if you do not stop writing for 30 seconds. Write anything that comes to mind, but keep writing. Stop writing immediately when the timer goes off. You don't have to write in complete sentences. You can write single words as well.

December Daily Gems

December 1

Beware of silent triggers. Triggers do not always make you feel profound sadness. Sometimes triggers can provoke other disturbing patterns, such as insomnia, binge-eating, excessive alcohol or drug use (including prescriptions), irritability, and even physical pain. When we make connections to how pain manifests itself in our lives, we are better positioned to control the outcome.

December 2

Someone understanding you is not the same as willingness to rescue you. Someone making you feel special is not a commitment to love you. Someone saying they love you does not make them responsible for your happiness. Embrace the exhilaration of the relationship from within. Know what the relationship is offering you in a way that you can feed yourself long-term. That way, if the person leaves, they will not take your joy with them.

December 3

There are no limits on the human spirit. Past trauma is not a determinant of future life experience, although it is a major influencer. We have words and concepts to identify the path we must take. Resilience, comeback, righteous rebellion, s/he who never gives up and does not settle for surviving. Although we may have felt like we were left for dead, we rise and fly again and again. We did not get here to stop. Here is only where you belong right now. There is where you are going. So, rest if you are weary but keep your eyes on the prize. Contemplate what is good and useful. When you do that, you will be contemplating on yourself.

December 4

The ego is the part of the psyche that focuses on information from the outside world and makes interpretations primarily based on the need to survive. All the unnecessary noise in your head comes from your ego's search for problems. Meditation, or quieting the mind, is so important to develop your authentic self instead of your reactionary ego. There is no direct path to the authentic self other than to quiet the ego. You quiet the ego by becoming the watcher.

December 5

Healing is difficult. Much of the work is isolating, emotionally painful, and turns your world upside down. It seems that discomfort is the only mode of transportation on the healing journey. There are times when dysfunction seems easier so we may turn back to addiction, abusive relationships, or sink into depression. These choices make us small as we crawl our way to death. Choosing to face our painful darkness leads us to life. The pain is real. The effort is tremendous. That is the only way that any thriver has gotten here. And even thriving is not pain-free. The pain just no longer frightens us or threatens to take us under. As we stop making choices that make us small, we become larger than the pain, so much larger.

December 6

Abandonment issues come in a variety, all with negative consequences on self and relationships. There is the *fear of abandonment*, which may lead you to overcompensate in relationships by giving too much, too soon in hopes that people will stay. There is the *resistance to abandonment* where you may overprotect yourself from abandonment by not allowing people to get close in the first place or by being the person who abandons relationships first at the earliest sign of discontent. There is the *distortion of abandonment* where even normal behaviors, such as work trips away, are perceived as a threat of abandonment. This usually results in a lot of unnecessary internal and external conflict. Then there is an *overreaction to abandonment* whereby any loss is a traumatic event, from pets dying to children leaving home, relationships ending, friends moving away, or even job loss. Pay attention to these patterns as you respond to the world.

December 7

Allowance, presence, sitting with things, and non-resistance easily sound like mumble-jumble because society does not foster these concepts. We learn to win, fight, resist, and conquer. So, healing puts us at odds with the status quo. This is one reason that relationships often fall apart on the healing path. If those relationships were upheld by traditional values, both partners have to be willing to shift. If you have a comfortable external life, you may have the most difficulty making the shift because the external comfort may serve as a great source of distraction. Usually, life has to remove the distraction of comfort to get us to shift and lean into the mumble-jumble. So, when things start to fall apart, commit to the shift.

December 8

Where there is fear, there is something that needs your internal attention more than an external response. Fear of failure may tell you that you are working from old scripts that no longer serve you. Fear of abandonment may warn you that you have given away too much personal power. Fear of being insignificant may be a whisper from your inner child to look within. So, the next time you feel that twinge of fear of the future, the unknown, or the uncontrollable, go within rather than acting from that place of fear. If you go within, you can make an internal shift to face the fear and respond to the world on your own terms.

December 9

Letting go of expectations allows the mystery of each moment to unfold. However, letting go of expectations does not mean you let go of your power. On the contrary, we let go of expectations to find our power. Instead of focusing on what someone else is giving, we focus on our ability to serve ourselves. Instead of putting all of our energy into hope, we put our energy into work—work on ourselves, for ourselves, about ourselves. We begin to create our own safe space and invite others into it. We can no longer invite others into a space of self-loathing and expect them to make us feel pretty or safe. But we can invite in the mystery of change and allow our lives to unfold as we watch and act on our own behalf.

December 10

There are many external approaches to healing that do not lead to satisfaction. We sometimes assume that there is one thing that will heal us and make the pain stop. We may, regrettably, target the perpetrator as a healing emphasis. Forgiving the perpetrator, confronting the perpetrator, punishing the perpetrator, or exposing the perpetrator keeps your focus on the perpetrator. Any of these actions may arise on the healing path as you process internally and focus on your inner child's needs. But these actions are sometimes forced as part of the dysfunctional response of looking externally for solutions.

December 11

The brain works mainly on a subconscious level to keep us alive. Its job is to get us used to our environment to increase our chances of survival. Repeated and consistent actions get coded as "normal." Keep in mind that normal is not a synonym for right, correct, or best. Normal means that the brain has adapted to the situation, behavior, or circumstance. The brain has picked up on a pattern. Once the brain picks up on a pattern, it protects the pattern by creating consistent experiences with the patterns. The good news is if you can hear yourself think, you can break the negative patterns.

December 12

Just because you have strong beliefs does not mean that they are true. Beliefs are simply the cognitive thoughts that we draw on to guide our behavior. Beliefs have little to do with truth. All people hold some beliefs that are not true. You may hold onto beliefs that are not true, even when the beliefs do not serve your best interest. We sometimes take on the beliefs of people from whom we seek love, even when those people hurt us. Much of our pain comes from our attachment to a belief that no longer serves us. Examination of our belief system is required on the healing journey.

December 13

For every action, there is a reaction. Rarely, if ever, does something good come into being without a compromise. Often, we let our desires get ahead of us without any consideration of consequences. We only focus on what good something is going to bring without making emotional space for the shift that usually comes with what we are asking for. A new car means less money to spend on your children, resulting in family problems. A baby means putting someone else's needs before yours in a way that may leave you physically and emotionally exhausted. So, we have to prepare for the consequences of our choices.

December 14

The best revenge is living well. Harm does not determine our outcome; we do. We either rebuild or remain stagnant. We practice new patterns or repeat the old ones. We embrace a story of victimization or design a life of resilience. Living well comes with pain, but the pain is purposeful. The residual pain of regret and trauma is replaced with the growing pangs of becoming transparent and living with authenticity. Our scars turn into stretch marks from reaching higher and bouncing back. One day, we wake up and accept that we are bigger than the trauma. This is "the good life" revenge.

December 15

Asking the right questions is essential on the healing journey. Most people look for answers, but the answer you seek is only as useful as the question that you ask. For example, asking how to heal is so broad that you are not likely to recognize an answer even if it comes. But asking yourself (your inner self), "What are my roadblocks to healing?" is a direct question. The question inherently calls your attention within. Ask questions that relate to self-responsibility rather than questions that focus on blame or expectation of others. The answer will likely require action or change or redirection from *you*. Then, we can begin to interact with the world to create our own destiny. Then, we are no longer victims.

December 16

When you operate from your power, people's actions have less influence on your emotional state. You make decisions based on your needs rather than making decisions that you believe will influence someone else's behavior. You expect their behavior will make you happy. Focusing on someone other than yourself disempowers you. You get to make decisions that make you happy when they are about you.

December 17

When desperation is in your heart, fear is in your mind. When fear is in your mind, victimization is in your path. When victimization is in your path, powerlessness is your perception. When powerlessness is in your perception, desperation is in your heart. You have to find a way to interfere with this cycle. Start by interrupting the cycle with intention. You already survived. You are no longer a victim.

December 18

The way to build a healthy social network is to pay attention to your behaviors that attract seemingly healthy people. Deal with your pain without the expectation of making therapists out of friends. You can have friends who do not want to listen to your issues. In fact, you *need* friends who are only in it to play with us. We need friends who can distract us. Those are, oftentimes, the people who remind us of our wholeness.

December 19

Your peak potential is on the other side of fear. So, walk through the door of judgment with your head held high. Sit at the feet of loneliness without regret. Bury the shame that was never yours to carry. Climb the mountain of rejection fiercely. Face the demons of doubt with determination. Act in the interest of self-love. You do not need to destroy your past. You just need to build your future.

December 20

Instead of playing hide and seek with our inner child, we can play heal-and-seek. The hide-and-seek mentality is a life of hiding the abuse from the world and hiding the effect of the abuse from yourself. When you do so, you seek affirmation, conformity, and acceptance. The heal-and-seek mentality is a life committed to healing the pain instead of hiding the pain. When you do so, you seek truth and authenticity.

When you find the truth of who you are, there will be no question about your lovability. Trusting becomes easier because we can always trust the truth of who we are. Hiding introduces us to a lot of lies, and choosing the best lie to distract us from pain is what gets us into a lot of trouble.

December 21

The dysfunction we lived with pushes us to look at life in very simplistic ways, keeping us unhappy and unhealthy. When dysfunction leads the way, life becomes black and white, either or. We call this "dichotomous thinking." Dichotomous thinking makes us miserable because we rarely get exactly what we want, leaving us to see only what we do not want. A dichotomous perspective always limits our view of our experiences. So, we must remain open to new ideas that do not represent the world the way that we have always seen it. Life is fluid. We must allow people to enter and exit without resentment. Nothing stays forever with the same degree of importance. Stop looking for stability and practice flexibility. Look for the gray in life. Welcome new lessons of growth. Learn how life looks from someone else's perspective. This, too, is related to healing.

December 22

So much of healing is the opposite of what we think. We think families should support us, but they often do not. We think we will immediately feel better, but we often feel worse at first. We expect our relationships to get better, but people leave instead. Often things fall apart, but that is often necessary for things to fall into place. So, try doing the opposite of what you are used to doing. Instead of holding on, let go. Instead of waiting for others to change, change yourself. Instead of hiding, live openly. Instead of giving up, dig your heels in. Sometimes, we have to let go of our programming to thrive. We just need daily practice and lots of trial and error.

December 23

The healing journey is a journey on which we say yes to pain. We heal a thousand times and prepare to heal again. We transform ourselves into the expression of self-love, and we move humanity forward by staying present. We live, and we learn. We accept and embrace. We let go of fear and become the light. We cannot do any of this in a day, week or year. We practice, practice, practice. We sleep with scars, bandage our bruises, tend to our aches, get up each day, and practice some more. We may have been the underdogs, but we're going for the championship.

December 24

We find ourselves on the healing journey for numerous reasons. Some people just want to stop feeling negative emotions. Others are in training to be a conduit of positive energy for the world. A sumo wrestler has a very different training regime than a gymnast. A golfer does not emphasize the same body development as a runner. So, we should ask ourselves what type of healing we are training for on our unique healing journeys.

December 25

Healing comes through commitment and sacrifice. However, you have to go within to know what to commit and sacrifice. The answers that move us forward are not what society tells you. There is so much to undo, unlearn, and let go of to get on the right track. The wrong track keeps you chasing ghosts, hoping for a rescue, wishing for acknowledgment of wrongdoing, seeking to be understood, or looking for a distraction. The wrong path expects you to remain silent and move on without addressing dysfunction. The healing path supports you to do the work to know thyself, "to thine own self be true."

December 26

Your healing intention must be authentic and transparent. Heal for the sake of healing. "For the sake of healing" means peaceful living, empowered living, purposeful living. When your intention to heal is focused on your need for a relationship to work out, your desire for work success, or to be liked or accepted by someone other than yourself, then part one of your healing work is working on your intention. You heal so that your life can change. That change may be your relationships, your work, or your purpose. Consequently, trying to hold onto what you have may be your greatest obstacle to healing. Healing with intention means that healing *is* the intention.

December 27

Perception and impact are quite specific to the individual. Our perception and impact are what we must each own. "You ignored me" is perception. "He tried to get me fired" is perception. "She didn't want to sit next to me" is perception. The impact that behavior has on us is based on our perception. Impact ownership always starts with "I felt." "I felt ignored by you," "I felt like he was trying to hurt me," and "I felt like she did not want to sit next to me" are statements of impact ownership. We can practice impact statements to sort out some of the feelings that we struggle with most often. This is how we begin to manage our feelings, as well as find our voice. Describing behavior, perception, and impact is an empowering exercise that we can practice for our personal growth.

December 28

Because of childhood trauma, many survivors live with an unhealthy balance of past, present, and future. Consequently, the mind is not efficient at predicting outcomes based on behavior. The mind ignores relevant information from the past or completely dismisses the future. Whatever the survivor consciously feels in the moment may be the only way they respond to the world. If they feel bad, they look to their immediate environment to blame. If they feel great, they look to their immediate environment for an explanation. They do not make connections between past, present, and future to create their lives. Restoring the balance between past, present, and future takes deep intention and a lot of trial and error over a long time, but it is surely possible. Don't limit your exploration of feelings to the immediate situation. Honor your past and how your emotions are attached to it.

December 29

The untraining, undoing, unlearning, backing up, turning around, and changing directions required for healing is exhausting, but we must learn what we need to let go and stop doing the things that are not working. Stop doing the things that repeatedly result in disappointment. If you have to choose between repeating an old pattern of pain or doing nothing, decide to do nothing at all and see what happens. New habits never arise while we are holding onto the old ones.

December 30

We have to train our hearts to live with brave truth instead of silent lies. Living bravely with truth requires practice. We hugely level up our resilience when we yield to the isolation that comes with truth-telling. When we commit to truth, we have to relearn most of what we thought we knew about the world. With our eyes open, we see that love was stated, but fear was practiced. 'Family' takes on a new meaning. Friends are temporary. And what is right often does not feel good. Doing the right thing sometimes leaves us with a feeling of emptiness. We fill up goodness only as we walk the narrow path of truth.

December 31

Shame hides within the crevices of our minds, not always at the forefront. Our negative feelings hang around for so long because we try to deny them. We hide them from ourselves, not just the world. All of our efforts to look healed prevent us from healing. Instead of our hearts becoming more authentic, our defenses just become more sophisticated. We learn to hide better instead of trust more. We learn to say the right thing instead of feeling the right thing. Yet, even this can be progress, as long as we know that there is more. There is more work to do if we want to embrace the life of authenticity and transparency that enables us to find strength through our vulnerability.

The Ultimate Healing Journey

Commit to the Journey

If the healing journey were easy, all survivors would be healed. Trauma is an assault on our humanity—physically, emotionally, and spiritually. We must use every fiber of being to find our way back to our most authentic, beautiful selves.

Healing is the journey through the portal to find our way back to our truest selves. We are creating notches in the lies we have come to believe about ourselves, others, and the world. We must turn over every stone in our heads and explore what is and is not useful in our living patterns and beliefs. We must commit to letting go of what holds us back, no matter how familiar.

The work is the work. There's no way around it. The less you engage in the work, the more pain will prevail. Here's a short list of ways to engage the work.

1) Commit to a virtual community that supports you. There is easy access to virtual communities. Don't dip in and out of the community based on how good you feel. Show up when you feel good *and* when you don't. You will find deeper healing when you show up to support others rather than only coming in when you need support. Commit because your community identity is part of the journey, not a pit stop.

You don't have to show up every day, or every week. But show up consistently.

2) Exercise your body. If you are physically able, there is no excuse. Do not give your mind the privilege of excuses. Your mind and body become disconnected due to trauma, and you have to restore the connection. An essential way to do this is with exercise that reconnects the mind and body, meaning the exercise is experienced as somewhat challenging but not dangerous.

3) Spend time in meditation, not just prayer. You can pray if that is your practice. But you must also meditate. Meditation is allowing the universe to speak to you. Prayer is you speaking to the universe. Find a meditation that you are comfortable with. There are zillions of them online. Do your due diligence and find one that works for you. This is independent work that you must do for yourself.

4) Write down or find someone you deeply trust to express everything that you are ashamed to release. Don't make public disclosure of it. Just find one way to get the trauma outside of yourself so that you can see it or hear it. You can even record it on your mobile phone. Don't do anything else with it yet. Just experience the release of having it outside of yourself.

5) Find your favorite guru of wellness. If that happens to be me, find all of my work, read it, watch it, follow it. If that's someone else, find all of their work, read it, watch it, follow it. Your guru should not only talk about trauma but about living well. We must learn what living well feels and looks like. Many survivors never had a chance to grow into a normal life. So, we have to learn about it and study it. Find your teacher.

6) Reread this book again and again. You will heal over time and the journey will become obscure now and again. Return to the book to resume your view.

If you commit to this lifestyle, you will no longer have the overwhelming feelings that come from trauma. You will begin your life of transformation.

CPSIA information can be obtained
at www.ICGtesting.com
Printed in the USA
LVHW010118110921
697560LV00018B/1766